Kate Freiligrath-Kroeker

A Century of German Lyrics

Kate Freiligrath-Kroeker

A Century of German Lyrics

ISBN/EAN: 9783744780124

Printed in Europe, USA, Canada, Australia, Japan

Cover: Foto ©Thomas Meinert / pixelio.de

More available books at **www.hansebooks.com**

A CENTURY OF GERMAN LYRICS

Uniform with this volume, price 3s. 6d.

LOVE SONGS
OF
ENGLISH POETS
1500-1800

WITH NOTES

By RALPH H. CAINE

LONDON: WILLIAM HEINEMANN

A CENTURY OF
GERMAN LYRICS

Selected, Arranged, and Translated

BY

KATE FREILIGRATH KROEKER

LONDON
WILLIAM HEINEMANN
1894

Dedication

Oh, Poets! you my well-loved Poets,
Who have gazed on me with your eyes immortal
From childhood upwards, first from my father's,
And now from my own study walls!
You know how I love you.
And if to-day I send you,
Send you with fear and trembling forth
In your new and untried garb,
I feel a flutter of soul,
And fain would I call you back
To add still a word or suppress another ;
Like unto an anxious mother
Who beholds her children departing from her.
But you list not my cry,
And have taken wing
For good and for worse ;
And you take no heed that for many years
You have sheltered with me,
Who now lose you reluctant.
But go! And for that I have loved you,
And have smiled and wept o'er you times without number,
Forgive me my sins and shortcomings,
And the poems I translated and did not translate,
You, my well-beloved Poets!

PREFACE

But few words are necessary to preface these Translations. I have to express my sincerest thanks to Baron Tauchnitz, as well as to Mr. Walter Scott, for their courteous permission to make use of my own versions, respectively, from the "Freiligrath Poems" in the Tauchnitz edition, and from the "Heine" of the Canterbury Series.

My father's fine poem, "The Dreadnought Hospital," is, however, not included in the Tauchnitz collection, having been subsequently translated by myself, and appearing in this volume for the first time with my other unpublished translations. The subject, one of peculiar interest to the English reader, is treated by the poet in his most characteristic vein, and I have always regretted that "Das Hospital Schiff" was not included amongst my father's poems until much later.

I am further indebted to Dr. Heinrich Vierordt for his kind permission to produce in English garb

Preface

his poem "Dioscuri," translated from the MS., and thus appearing here before the original has been published in Germany.

In conclusion, I may still remark that, while I trust the alphabetical index of authors with dates may prove of use and interest to the reader, the sequence of poets in the volume itself is chronological.

K. F. K.

CONTENTS

	PAGE
ARNIM, ACHIM VON. (1781-1831)	
A Prayer	11
BECK, KARL. (1817-1879)	
Resignation	176
CHAMISSO, ADALBERT VON. (1781-1833)	
The Castle of Boncourt	12
DAHN, FELIX. (1834)	
Kriemhild	218
Hagen's Death Song	220
DROSTE-HÜLSHOF, ANNETTE VON. (1797-1848)	
The Boy on the Moor	50
The Deserted House	52
EICHENDORFF, JOSEPH VON. (1788-1857)	
The Loreley	22
On the Death of my Child	23
Moonlit Night	23
FREILIGRATH, FERDINAND. (1810-1876)	
Sea Fable	127
Roland	129
The Flowers' Revenge	132
On the Sea	136
The Death of the Leader	138
The Water Gueux	141
Henry	144

Contents

FREILIGRATH, FERDINAND. (1810-1876)—*continued*.   PAGE
- The Fir-tree 145
- Africa 149
- Leviathan 155
- The Dreadnought Hospital 158
- On the Drachenfels 163
- Wild Flowers 164
- A Hamlet on the Rhine 167
- The Trumpet of Gravelotte 172

GEIBEL, EMMANUEL. (1815-1884)
- In April 175

GOETHE, JOHANN WOLFGANG VON. (1749-1832)
- Gipsy Song 1
- Night Thoughts 2
- Reconciliation 3
- My Goddess 4
- Song of the Parcæ (from "Iphigencia") . . . 7
- Charon. (From the new Greek) 9
- The Critic 10

GRILLPARZER, FRANZ. (1790-1872)
- To the Tragic Muse 25

GROTH, KLAUS. (1819)
- He Talked, Oh so Much 182
- Old Büsum. (Folk Lore) 183
- He Woke. (Folk Lore) 184
- The Haunted Moor. (Folk Lore) . . . 185
- The Haunted House. (Folk Lore) . . . 186
- The Holy Oak. (Folk Lore) 187
- The Knotted Stick. (Folk Lore) . . . 189
- Hans Iwer. (Folk Lore) 192

HAMERLING, ROBERT. (1832-1888)
- The Incantation of the Dead 205

HARTMANN, MORITZ. (1821-1872)
- Bulgarian Lament 197

Contents

HEINE, HEINRICH. (1799-1856)   PAGE

E'en as a lovely flower	55
As the moon bursts forth in splendour	55
What means this lonely tear-drop	56
I gazed upon her picture	57
We sat at the fisherman's cottage	58
How canst thou sleep so softly	59
At the cross-roads he lies buried	60
Your white slender lily fingers	60
Down fall and flutter sadly	61
Around the garden I wander	61
The midnight hour was drear and cold	62
The Message	62
Dimly sinks the summer evening	63
Night lies on the silent highways	63
Almansor	64
Soft and gently through my soul	69
The butterfly is in love with the rose	69
Was once an ancient monarch	70
With gloomy sails my ship doth fly	70
Too late come now your smiles of promise	71
Katharine	72
Desist!	72
Heinrich	73
Rude mediæval barbarism	74

THE NORTH SEA.

First Part.

Coronation	75
Twilight	76
Sunset	77
Night on the Beach	79
Poseidon	82
Declaration	84
At Night in the Cabin	85
Storm	88
Ocean Calm	90
Sea Vision	91
Cleansing	94
Peace	95

Contents

HEINE, HEINRICH. (1799-1856)—*continued*.

THE NORTH SEA.
Second Part.
	PAGE
Good Morrow	97
The Thunderstorm	99
Shipwreck	100
The Setting Sun	102
Song of the Oceanides	104
The Gods of Greece	108
Questions	111
The Phœnix	112
In the Harbour	114
Epilogue	116

HEYSE, PAUL. (1830)

The Valley of the Espingo	202

KELLER, GOTTFRIED. (1819-1890)

Woodland Song	177
My bright eyes are shining	178
By Flowing Waters	179
Winter Night	181

LENAU, NICOLAUS. (1802-1850)
Sedge Songs:
Faintly sets the sun o'er yonder	118
Oft at eve I love to saunter	119
Angry sunset sky	119
Mist	120

LINGG, HERMANN. (1820)

The Black Death	194

MOERIKE, EDUARD. (1804-1875)

One little hour ere Day	125
Suum Cuique	126

MOSEN, JULIUS. (1803-1867)

The Crossbill	121

Contents

MÜLLER, WILHELM. (1794-1827)   PAGE

    (CYCLE OF SONGS: THE WINTER JOURNEY.)

Good-night	28
The Weather Vane	29
Frozen Tears	30
Frozen	30
The Linden Tree	31
Thaw	33
On the River	33
Looking Back	34
The Will-o'-the-Wisp	35
Rest	36
Spring Dreams	37
Solitude	38
The Post	39
The Gray Head	39
The Crow	40
The Last Hope	40
In the Village	41
The Stormy Morning	42
Illusion	42
The Sign Post	43
The Inn	44
Defiance	44
The Rival Suns	45
The Organ Grinder	45

PLATEN, AUGUST GRAF VON. (1795-1835)

The Pilgrim before St. Just	47
A Winter Sigh	48
Winter Song	48
Lot of the Lyrist	48

RITTERSHAUS, EMIL. (1834)

On the Battlefields of Metz	213
I asked the Sun	217

Contents

RÜCKERT, FRIEDERICH. (1788-1866)   PAGE

    The Dying Flower 16

        CHILD DIRGES, I., II., III.:

    Human death and human life 19
    A shadow in the daytime 20
    I had fondly hoped, my little daughter . . . 21

SCHEFFEL, VICTOR VON. (1826-1888)

    Heini of Steier 200

UHLAND, LUDWIG. (1787-1862)

    The King on the Tower 14
    On the Death of a Child 15
    On the Death of a Country Parson 15

VIERORDT, HEINRICH. (1855)

    Cupid's Market 223
    Dioscuri 224

Johann Wolfgang von Goethe

Gipsy Song

IN drizzling fog, in the deep, deep snow,
In forest wild, in the winter night,
I heard the barking of hungry wolves,
I heard the shrieking of owls:
   Wille wow wow wow!
   Wille wo wo wo!
   Wito hoo!

I shot a cat by the garden fence,
'Twas the pet black cat of Ann, the witch;
That night seven were-wolves came to my bed,
Seven village cronies were they:
   Wille wow wow wow!
   Wille wo wo wo!
   Wito hoo!

I knew them all, I knew them well—
Old Ursula, Ann, and Kate,
And Barbara, Meg, and Lizzy, and Bess—
They glared in a circle and howled:
  Wille wow wow wow!
  Wille wo wo wo!
  Wito hoo!

Then loudly each by her name I called:
What want you here? You, Ann? You, Bess?
Then shook they all over and tossed their heads,
And, howling, they fled away.
  Wille wow wow wow!
  Wille wo wo wo!
  Wito hoo!

Night Thoughts

YOU I pity, hapless stars and distant,
You so fair and you so sweetly shining,
Gladly showing light to anxious sailors,
And by gods and men still unrewarded.
For ye love not, never knew sweet passion!
Irresistibly, the hours eternal
Lead you onwards through the spacious heavens.
What dread circuits you've but now accomplished,
Whilst I, in the arms of my Beloved,
You and Midnight have alike forgotten.

Reconciliation

(From the "Trilogy of Passion")

PASSION brings pain! Ah, who shall soothe the aching,
Who soothe the heart, bereft of all it lost?
Where are those hours, so blissful in the waking?
In vain was yours all that you treasured most!
Dimmed is the mind, confused all you are trying;
The world so fair, fast from your view is flying.

Then, Music, lo! on angel-wings down soaring,
A million tones to one doth intertwine,
And in man's heart her magic full outpouring,
His bosom fills with beauty's beam divine;
The eye gleams wet, and feels in fervent yearning
The god-like worth of Sound and Teardrops burning.

And so the heart, free from its pain, discovers
That still it lives and beats, and joys to beat;
And in reward, e'en as do happy lovers,
Offers itself as in thanksgiving meet.
'Tis then you feel—oh, may it ne'er be blighted!—
The twainfold bliss of Sound and Love united.

My Goddess

Which of the Immortals
Shall claim the highest prize?
I contend with no one,
But I will give it
To the ever-changing,
Ever new,
Strangest daughter of Jove;
To his favourite child
Fair Phantasy.

For he allows her
All those caprices
Which he himself only
Is wont to enjoy;
And he regards
With paternal pleasure
His darling's antics.

Whether, rose-crowned,
With wand of lilies,
She trip it o'er flowery meads,
Reigning o'er birds of summer,
And sipping light dew
From buds and blossoms
With honey lips;

Or, whether she rave
With streaming hair,
And gloomy-eyed,
On the wings of the wind,
O'er mountain summits;
Appearing to mortals
Rainbow-hued,
Now like morn and evening,
Anon like trembling moonbeams,
But ever varying:

Let us sing praises
All to the Father,
Our great, ancient Father,
To Him who has given
This fair and unfading
Companion as wife.

For to us only
Hath he espoused her
In bonds celestial,
And hath enjoined her,
As faithful consort,
Ne'er to take flight
In joy or in sorrow.

For all the other
Grovelling races
Of our fruitful mother,
The teeming Earth,

Grope on darkly
In the blind enjoyment
Of the present moment,
And the troubled burden
Of their narrow life,
Bent low by the yoke
Of Necessity.

But to us grants He
His brightest daughter,
His dearest spoiled child.
Rejoice, O mankind!
Meet her lovingly
E'en as a Beloved;
Render her honour
Due to a wife.

And, look you, take heed
That old grandmother Wisdom
Do not offend
My shy, sensitive child!

But I know, too, her elder
Sedater sister,
My quiet companion and friend;
Ah, may she only
With my life leave me,
The noble Encourager,
Comforter—Hope!

Song of the Parcæ

(From "Iphigeneia")

LET mortals fear humbly
The gods up on high !
They hold their dread power
In hands sempiternal,
And ever they use it
As pleases to them.

Let him fear them doubly
Whome'er they exalted !
On clouds and on quicksands
Stand tables and benches
Prepared, all of gold.

If strife e'er arises,
The guests are hurled headlong,
Reviled and dishonoured,
To abysses nocturnal ;
And there await vainly,
In darkness fast-fettered,
On righteous fair sentence.

But they remain ever
At banquets eternal,
At spread golden tables.

They stride the abysses,
From mountain to mountain;
From bottomless chasms
The hot breath of Titans,
Deep smothered and stifled,
Steams into their nostrils,
Like sweet-smelling incense,
A pleasant light vapour!

The gods will turn often
Their joy-bringing glances
From whole generations;
Nor care to remember
The ancestor's features,
Once loved and still pleading
In eloquent silence,
In those of his grandson.

Thus sang the dread Sisters:—
In banishment gloomy
And cavern nocturnal
The exile doth hear them,
And listeth their singing;
He thinks of his children
And shakes his hoar head.

Charon

(From his Translation of New Greek Songs)

WHY are the mountain-tops so black?
Whence comes yon misty vapour?
Is it the stormwind battling there,
Or rain, the summits beating?
'Tis not the stormwind raging high,
Nor rain the summits beating;
'Tis Charon dread, who sweeps along,
The Dead all with him hurrying;
The young he drives before him fast,
The old he drags behind him,
The youngest, tender infants they,
Are strung upon his saddle.
The old men call on him to stop,
The youths kneel down beseeching:
"Oh, Charon, stop! Stop at the hedge!
Stop at the crystal fountain!
The old may there refresh themselves,
The young may there disport them,
The tender children roam about
To cull the bright-hued flowers."

"Not at the green hedge will I stop,
Nor at the crystal fountain;

The women would fetch water there,
And recognize their children;
Her husband, too, would each one know—
Impossible to part them."

The Critic

A FELLOW dined with me t'other day,
He wasn't exactly in my way;
I was sitting down to my usual dinner,
To repletion guttled the hungry sinner;
My desert he by no means did despise,
And scarce is the fellow full up to his eyes,
Than the devil must lead him next door full fast
To grumble there at my poor repast:
" The soup might have been more rich, I opine,
The joint more tender, fuller-bodied the wine!"
Confound the rapscallion! He raises my bile!
Strike him dead, the dog! He's a Critic vile!

Achim von Arnim

A Prayer

Oh grant me love, and a glad heart bestow,
That I may sing Thee, Lord of all below.

With joyous health a careless ease give me,
A pious heart, and courage bold and free.

Grant children, Lord, worthy our love and care,
All enemies far from the threshold scare.

Next grant me wings; and last, a mound of sand,
That mound of sand in my dear fatherland.

The wings give to my soul, that yearns to stay,
That it may tear itself from earth away!

Adalbert von Chamisso

The Castle of Boncourt

I DREAM myself back to my childhood
    And shake my hoary head,
Why haunt me thus, ye visions
    That I long thought forgotten and dead?

From verdant shade there uprises
    A castle in stately pride,
Well know I those pinnacled towers,
    The bridge and the gateway beside.

The lions upon the escutcheon
    Look down with familiar face,
I greet my old friends and companions,
    And haste up the courtyard apace.

The sphinx by the well lies yonder,
    All green doth the fig-tree gleam,
And yonder, behind those windows,
    I once dreamed my first dream.

Chamisso

I enter the castle chapel
    And seek my forefathers' grave;
'Tis here, there hangs the old armour,
    The tattered old banners wave.

My tear-dimmed eyes are trying
    To read the inscription in vain,
What though the light from the windows
    Breaks full through the coloured pane.

Thus firmly, oh house of my fathers,
    Remainest thou fixed on my heart,
The harrow and ploughshare pass o'er thee,
    No longer on earth thou art.

Oh cherished soil, be thou fruitful,
    I lovingly bless thee now,
And bless him doubly whoever
    Shall over thee drive his plough.

But I from my dreams will arouse me,
    My harp within my hand;
And o'er the wide world go roaming,
    Singing from land to land.

Ludwig Uhland

The King on the Tower

THERE do they all lie, reposing soft,
The mountains grey, and the darkling lea;
Now slumber reigns, and the breezes waft
No sound of lament to me.

For all have I worked, I have striven for all,
With care have I drunk the sparkling wine;
But now at length I will gladden my soul,
For Night has descended, the calm, the divine.

Oh, ye letters of gold through the starry space,
To you I gaze up with longing and love;
Oh, mysterious strains that are audible scarce,
How you wistfully whisper mine ear from above.

Mine eye is dim and my hair is white,
In my hall hang victoriously armour and crest;
I have faithfully spoken and practised the Right,
Oh, when may I slumber and rest?

Oh, blessed Repose, how I long for thee,
Oh, resplendent Night, why delay you so long?
When the brighter rays of the stars I shall see,
And hear a far fuller song!

On the Death of a Child

You came, you went, as angels go,
A fleeting guest within our land.
Whence and where to?—We only know:
Forth from God's hand into God's hand.

On the Death of a Country Parson

If spirits, once departed, ever may
Visit again the cheerful realms of day,
Then wilt thou not return when pale moonbeams
Awaken tender melancholy dreams;
But on some sunny morn, when up on high
Not e'en a cloudlet flecks the deep blue sky,
When nodding harvests raise their golden head
All interspersed with flowers blue and red:
Then wilt thou roam the fields as erst awhile,
And greet each reaper with a gentle smile.

Friederich Rückert

The Dying Flower

Hope! thou yet shalt live to see
Spring returning fresh and fair;
Hope inspires every tree
Which rude autumn winds stripped bare;
Hoping with the silent strength
Of its buds through winter drear,
Till the sap shall burst at length,
And new foliage crown the year.

" Ah! no mighty tree am I,
O'er which thousand summers wing,
After long sad winter dream
Weaving fresh new poems of spring;
I am but the flower, alas,
Wakened by May's genial glow,
Of which nothing shall remain
Once 'tis covered deep with snow."

Rückert

Then, if thou art but the flower,
Thou of heart so meek and low,
Comfort take, for seed is given
To all things that bloom below;
Let death's tempest's chilly blast
Thy life ashes roughly strew,
From this very dust shalt thou
Hundredfold thyself renew!

"Truly, others after me
In my likeness shall arise,
Nature's verdure lasts for aye,
But in detail quickly dies;
Yet, if they are what I was,
I myself exist no more,
Only now am I myself,
Ne'er again and ne'er before.

"When the sun shall kindle them,
Which yet thrills me warm and bright,
Can that soothe the bitter fate
Which condemns me soon to night?
Even now, oh fickle sun,
Thou dost turn to them I see,
Wherefore still with frosty smile
Art thou falsely mocking me?

"Woe's me, that I trusted thee,
Wooed, kissed open by thy ray;

That I gazed into thine eye
Till it stole my life away!
To withdraw this life's poor rest
From thy pity hard and cold,
I will hide myself from thee,
All my petals close I'll fold.

" But my anger's stubborn ice
Thou dost melt, my tears now run—
Take, oh take my fleeting life
Up to thee, eternal sun!
Thou with sunny smile dost chase
From my soul all gloom and pain,
—All I e'er received from thee,
Dying, I'd acknowledge fain.

" Every morning breeze that swayed
My frail stem one summer's space,
Every butterfly that played,
Glancing round in airy race;
Bright eyes, gladdened by my hue,
Hearts, cheered by my fragrant power—
As thou subtly wroughtest me,
Sun, I thank thee in this hour.

" Of thy world an ornament,
Be it ne'er so humbly low,
Like the stars in higher spheres,
Thou didst let me blush and glow;

One last breath I'll fondly draw,
And it shall not be a sigh,
One look on the beauteous earth,
One last gaze upon the sky.

"Thou, the world's great heart of flame,
Let me wither 'neath thy ray,
Heaven, spread thy azure tent,
Whilst I fade and pass away.
Hail, to thee oh radiant spring!
Hail, soft breeze, hail summer's rain!
Without grief I fall asleep,
Without hope to rise again.

Child Dirges

I.

HUMAN death and human life
Is a riddle!
What the fates are calmly weaving
Is a riddle.

That ye were unto me given
Is a wonder;
That again I must restore you
Is a riddle.

That you live to me in death still
Is a marvel,
And my life, since I have lost you,
Is a riddle.

II.

A shadow in the daytime,
A flame by night thou art;
Thou livest in my sorrow,
Nor diest in my heart.

Where'er I build my dwelling,
Close to my side dost start;
Thou livest in my sorrow,
Nor diest in my heart.

Where'er I ask of thee, child,
Comes answer every part,
Thou livest in my sorrow,
Nor diest in my heart.

A shadow in the daytime
A flame by night thou art;
Thou livest in my sorrow,
Nor diest in my heart.

Rückert

III.

I had fondly hoped, my little daughter,
That thou shouldst have stayed with thy old father,
Never to have left him, while thy brothers
Roamed about the world their fortune seeking,
From their parents' hearts they torn asunder;
I had pictured thee around thy mother,
Doing what was play, anon in earnest;
And I saw thee bring my sweetened coffee,
As she brought it erst, by thee attended.
And behold! now dost thou bring this bitter,
Bitter draught, and I, woe's me, must drink it.
To take off the bitterness I tell me,
Not for ever wouldst thou have remained;
Unawares there would have come a suitor
And thy little heart had throbbed to meet him,
While I should have said perforce: Come in, then!
And the youthful wedded wife her husband
Would have better loved than her old father,
And her children better still than either!
For that more than all you love your children,
I now learn, alas, when I have lost you!
Now, thou savest me this pang of anguish,
Little daughter, and canst love thy father,
Solely, fondly, as he thee doth cherish.

Joseph Freiherr von Eichendorff

The Loreley

"'Tis late already, late and cold,
Why ride you lonely through the wold?
The wood is drear, alone you roam,—
Fair maid, I'll bear you with me home."

"Great is man's guile and subtle art,
With grief is broken my poor heart;
Faint sounds the bugle, high and low,
Ah, fly, ere who I am you know!"

"How richly decked the rider and her steed,
How fair those tender limbs do plead;
I know you now! God be my stay!
You are the sorceress Lorcley!"

"You know me well, and well you know
My castle frowning dark below;
'Tis late already, late and cold,
You nevermore shall leave this wold!"

On the Death of my Child

The clocks strike in the distance,
   'Tis midnight's deepest shade;
The lamp is dimly burning,
   Thy little bed is made.

Only the wind is sobbing
   Around our cottage drear,
We sit in lonely silence,
   Listening with anxious ear.

Methinks we still must hear thee
   Tap gently at the door,
As though from weary wandering
   Thou didst return footsore.

We poor deluded mortals,
   In darkness yet we roam,
While thou hast long since gainéd
   Thy calm eternal home.

A Moonlit Night

Methought the heavens had wafted
   Down to the earth a kiss,
Which she on her blossom-pillow
   Now dreams of with thrills of bliss.

The night wind passed o'er the meadows
   The cornfields swayed in the air,
The forest gently murmured,
   The night was so starlit and fair.

Then shook my soul her pinions
   Wide open, far to roam
O'er the dim silent country,
   As though 'twere flying home.

Franz Grillparzer

To the Tragic Muse

(Written on finishing his Tragedy of "Medea")

HOLD, Gloomy one, nor farther go!
Where do you lure me on?
Over mountains have I toiled after,
Have followed you over chasms;
No path whereon to tread, no human track,
Men's voices dimly sound from afar,
Sounds, too, the cheerful tinkling of herds,
And the roaring torrent;
Around me rocks, cloud-kissing rocks,
On high, mist and vapour,
Aping man's semblance!

What will you? Stand and tell me!—
Lo, at your side a woman
Of terrible aspect:
Her swarthy hair flutters,

Her black eyes glitter,
Her garment is black !—Lo,
Blood upon her garment,
On the dagger she draws !

Dead at her feet lie two children,
And a young and old man,
Distorting in death-anguish
Consanguine similar features ;
And round her shoulders is shimmering
The Fleece—the gold-flashing Fleece !—Medea !

Get you from hence, dread Murderess
Of children, of brother and father !
What have I in common with you ?
I have reverently honoured my father,
And when my mother died
My pious tears flowed
On her early unwished-for grave !—
What have I in common with you ?
I shudder. Depart !

And you, too, you, who lured me on,
With the lyre within your arm,
With the garland you wear
Of undying bays that allure me,
Get you hence, too, and leave me,
That I, groping my way back,
May return to my people.

But, lo, you bend on me
That glance, at once severe and tender,
That soul-searching glance of yours
Which already, when but a boy,
Took out of his hand his playthings,
And withdrawing him from his companions,
Banished him into solitude,
And gave him to ponder
The fate of monarchs,
And the world's unsolved and eternal riddles,
As presaging, thoughtful diversion.

You still gaze on me, and will not go?
I am to follow you, yourself and companion,
Medea of the terrible eye?
You take your garland from off your own,
And place it upon the Dread one's brow?
For me yon glory?   For me yon reward?
You still smile and beckon?
I am to follow, to be rewarded?
My spirit is not proof against such weapons!
Your arrows, lo, are transfixed in my breast!
Completed be what I begun!
Beckon no longer, for you have conquered;
Lead on !   I will follow.

Wilhelm Müller

THE WINTER JOURNEY

Good-Night

As stranger I came hither,
As stranger I depart ;
With blooms that never wither
Spring stole into my heart.
The maiden said, "I love you !"
The mother, "You must wed !"
Now is the world so dreary,
Snow-clouds loom dark o'erhead.

I cannot choose the season
When I go forth from here,
Myself must seek my pathway
All in this darkness drear ;
The moon, as my companion,
Flits by me, dim and pale,
And ever I go searching
O'er whitened hill and dale.

Why should I tarry yonder
Until they drove me hence?
Let stray dogs go a-howling
Before their master's fence.
Love likes to roam and wander,
For such is his delight,
From this one to another—
Good-night, Sweetheart, good-night!

I'll not disturb your dreams, dear,
'Twere pity for your sleep;
You shall not hear my footsteps,
Adown the stairs I'll creep.
I'll just write on the door, dear,
" Good-night," ere I depart,
That you may see to-morrow,
I've thought of you, Sweetheart!

The Weather Vane

THE wind plays wildly with the silly
Bright weather vane on her abode;
And lo, methought 'twas mocking shrilly
The poor sad traveller in the road.

Ah! sooner far should he have heeded
The symbol of the house displayed,
And never had he then expected,
Inside a true and constant maid.

With my poor heart the wind is playing,
As on the roof, but not so loud :
What care these people for my sorrow,
Their child will marry, rich and proud.

Frozen Tears

COLD icy drops are falling
   Down from my cheeks full slow;
And have I then been weeping?
   How is't I did not know!

Oh teardrops, bitter teardrops,
   Wherefore so cold are you,
That all to ice you're frozen
   Like chilly morning's dew?

Yet from my heart upwelling
   You gush with fervid woe,
As though you'd fain be melting
   All winter's ice and snow.

Frozen

I SEEK her footstep's traces
   In this deep snow in vain,
Where to my arm close clinging,
   She roamed the verdant plain.

I'll melt the ground with kisses,
   I'll pierce through ice and snow
With tears all hot and burning,
   Till I see earth below.

Where shall I find a blossom,
   Where find a blade of green?
The flowers all are frozen,
   The grass is dull of sheen.

Shall I then take no token
   From hence, no memory?
When all my woes are silent,
   Who'll speak of her to me?

My heart is dead and frozen,
   Cold lies her image there;
Should e'er my heart be thawed again,
   That, too, will fade in air.

The Linden Tree

A LINDEN tree grows blithely
   Out by the village well;
How oft I've dreamed beneath it
   Sweet dreams, I scarce can tell.

Into its bark I've graven
   Full many a well-loved name,
It ever drew me onwards,
   In joy and grief the same.

To-day I had to pass it
   Beneath drear midnight skies,
And even in that darkness
   I fain had closed mine eyes.

And lo, its branches murmured
   As calling unto me :
"Come hither, ah, come hither,
   Here is repose for thee !"

The bitter blast was blowing
   Full in my face anon,
It caught my hat and whirled it—
   I steadfastly went on.

Now many a weary hour
   I'm absent from my tree,
And still I hear it murmur :
   "You'll find repose with me !"

Thaw

MANY a tear has fallen blindly
   From mine eyes on to the snow,
Thirstily the flakes absorb them,
   Drinking in my fervid woe.

When the buds begin to burgeon,
   Warm mild airs begin to blow,
And the ice breaks up in thunder,
   And all softly melts the snow.

Snow, thou knowest of my yearning,
   Tell me, whither wends thy way?
Only follow thou my teardrops,
   Soon they'll join the brooklet gay.

You will roam the town together,
   In and out each busy street,—
When my tears you shall feel burning,
   There have passed my Dear one's feet!

On the River

OH, bright and cheery river,
   That rushed so swiftly by,
How hushed art thou and silent,
   With never a last good-bye.

With ice hast thou encrusted
    Thy surface, thick and strong;
Rigid and without motion
    Winds thy cold length along.

With sharpest stone I've graven
    Upon thy surface dour,
The name of my Beloved,
    The day and very hour :

The day of our first meeting,
    The hour I went again,
And round the name and number
    A ring that's broke in twain.

My heart, dost in this river
    Thy image, haply, know?
I wonder if beneath it
    Swells, too, such raging woe !

Looking Back

I CHAFE and burn with hot impatience
    Although I face an icy wind,
Fain would I ne'er draw breath nor rest me
    Till every house was left behind.

Against each stone I've knocked and stumbled
  In my wild haste from out the town,
From all the eaves the snowballs crumbled,
  That mocking crows were flinging down.

Far differently you once received me,
  Oh town of sad inconstancy,
Before your windows bright were singing
  Song-birds in rival melody.

The fragrant limes were sweetly blowing,
  The fountains plashed in summer shine,
And ah, two soft kind eyes were glowing—
  Then wast thou done for, heart of mine!

Whene'er that day I now remember
  I fain would backwards gaze once more,
And fain would I return, all faltering,
  And stand again beside her door.

The Will-o'-the-Wisp

To the wilderness you've lured me
  Will-o'-the-wisp, full fair to see;
How an egress to discover
  Does not greatly trouble me;

Used am I to stray and wander,
   To one goal leads every way;
All our joys and all our sorrows
   Are but Jack-o'-lantern's play.

Down the mountain stream's dry channel
   Calm I wend, through rocks and gloom,—
Every stream must gain the ocean,
   Every sorrow find its tomb.

Rest

Now that I lay me down to rest,
   All worn I feel and weary;
Throughout the day I have kept up
   O'er lonely roads and dreary.

My feet nor asked for halt or rest,
   The sharp cold kept me going,
The stormwind eased my weary back,
   And helped me onwards, blowing.

Into a humble wayside hut
   For rest I fain am turning,
But ah, my limbs can find no rest,
   So sore their wounds are burning.

Thou too, my heart, so fierce and bold,
    Tempest and storm defying;
Lo, in this calm, dost feel but now
    Thy canker's worm undying!

Spring Dreams

I DREAMED of sweet bright flowers,
    Of bloom and blossom in May,
I dreamed of spring-green meadows,
    Of birds singing blithely and gay.

And when the cock crowed shrilly,
    The dream fled from mine eye,
And all was dark and dreary,
    I heard the night-raven's cry.

Say, who upon my windows
    Traced fairy flower and tree?
Ye smile perchance at the dreamer
    Who flowers in winter doth see!

I dreamed of a sweet bright maiden,
    Of rapturous love and bliss,
Of vows and lover's caresses,
    Of many a burning kiss.

And when the cock crowed shrilly
   My heart woke with a moan,
And now I sadly ponder
   On my sweet dream alone.

I softly close my eyelids,
   My heart still throbs so warm—
Ye frost flowers, when will ye blossom?
   When shall I clasp thee in my arm?

Solitude

LIKE to a cloud, that gloomy
   Floats through a smiling sky,
When in the pine-trees' summit
   A faint soft breeze goes by:

Thus I drag on my journey
   With listless foot and slow;
Lonely and without greeting,
   Through gladsome life I go.

Ah, bright and radiant heavens,
   Bright without cloud or blot,
Whilst yet the storms were raging
   So wretched was I not!

The Post

From the street below the post-horn sounds,
Why is it that it so starts and bounds,
  My heart?

No letter brings the post for me,
Why beat you then so furiously,
  My heart?

Ah sooth, the post comes from the town,
Where a fair love I called my own,
  My heart!

Shall I run over just to see,
And ask how all with her may be,
  My heart?

The Gray Head

Jack Frost has grizzled o'er my hair
 With silvery sheen and hoary;
I smiled to think I had grown old,
 Rejoicing at the story.

But soon it melted all away,
 No more my curls are whitened;
How far still to the grave, ah say!—
 Of my own youth I'm frightened!

From even unto morning sun
   Men have turned old and weary;
And lo, my hair has not turned white
   In all this journey dreary.

The Crow

Yon black crow has followed me
   From the town, before me;
Still my head encircling, he
   Day by day flies o'er me.

Tell me, Crow, fantastic bird,
   Wilt thou ne'er forsake me?
Dost thou think to seize me soon,
   On my blood to slake thee?

Well, this journey soon is o'er,
   To the grave I'm wending;
Crow, let me at length behold
   Constancy unending!

The Last Hope

Here and there, a leaf is hanging,
   Left a-hanging on the trees,
And I often watch it swaying,
   Fluttering in the fitful breeze.

On that leaf I gaze and ponder,
   Fix my hope on it so sere ;
When the wind plays with my leaflet,
   Then I tremble, too, with fear.

Ah, and when to earth it falleth,
   Sinks my hope with it along,
Lo, myself to earth am falling,
   On its grave sad-weeping long.

In the Village

The dogs are barking, their chains loud rattling,
While men lie abed with dreams sore battling ;
Dreaming of things which they never have had,
Taking their fill both of good and of bad,
Lo, and all's fled at the dawn of the morrow.—
Ah well, they have shared of joy and of sorrow,
And hope the rest they have left behind
Upon their pillows again to find.

Let me not rest, ye watch-dogs trusty,
Furiously drag at your chains so rusty ;
Behold, I have done with dreams for ever,
So let me, too, from yon slumberers sever.

The Stormy Morning

How has the tempest riven
    Heaven's sombre robe of gray!
Spent, tattered clouds are drifting
    About in weak affray.

And tongues of lurid fire
    Between them flash and dart—
Oh, how a stormy morning,
    Like this, doth love my heart!

Its own reflected picture
    It therein can discern—
'Tis nothing but grim winter,
    Grim winter, wild and stern!

Illusion

A DANCING light doth cheer my way,
I follow it—and go astray;
I gladly follow, though aware
That it is but a dazzling snare.
Ah, who so wretched e'en as I,
Loves to believe such radiant lie,

That shows, 'mid ice and snow and gloom,
Delusively, a bright warm home,
And in that home my darling see!—
Illusion is the best for me!

The Sign-Post

Why avoid the beaten highway,
   Which all other travellers go,
Seeking hidden path and byway,
   Rocky solitudes and snow?

I have done nor wrong nor evil
   To evade my fellow-men—
Say, what foolish whim and fancy
   Drives me forth to desert glen?

Finger-posts stand by the wayside,
   Pointing to the distant town,
And I journey on and onward
   Seeking rest and finding none.

Lo, a Sign-post I see standing,
   Fixed, unmoved, upon my track,
And a road I have to journey,
   Road, from which none e'er comes back!

The Inn

INTO a country churchyard
  Hath led me on my way;
Here will I stop and rest me,
  I to myself did say.

Ye green funereal garlands
  Are sign-boards of this inn,
That tempt the weary traveller
  To stay and rest within.

Are then, inside, these chambers
  Bespoken one and all?
I am so faint and footsore,
  I'm wounded like to fall.

Oh, unkind Inn and cheerless,
  Wherefore refuse my quest?
Toil onward, still, toil onwards,
  My faithful staff, nor rest.

Defiance

WHEN the snow drives in my face,
  Lightly off I fling it;
When my heart in sorrow moans,
  Lightly off I sing it;

Will not listen what it tells,
    All its sighs heed never;
Turn deaf ear to its complaints—
    Fools are plaining ever.

Bravely onwards, ever on,
    'Gainst all wind and weather,
If no gods on earth there be,
    We'll be gods together.

The Rival Suns

BLAZING beheld I three suns on high,
I gazed on them long and steadfastly;
And they, too, stared so fixedly,
As if they would not part from me.
Alas, *my* suns ye three are not,
For you on others gaze, I wot!
Ah, I had three the other day,
Now the two best have passed away.
Would that the third set too, so stark,—
I should feel better in the dark.

The Organ Grinder

LISTEN to yon crazy,
    Poor old organ-man,
With his stiff numb fingers
    Grinding all he can.

Barefoot, see him tottering
  On the icy plain,
While his little platter
  Empty doth remain.

No one cares to hear him,
  No one looks his way,
And the dogs go growling
  Round him in fierce play.

And he lets things happen
  Even as they will,
Turns his wheezy organ,
  Never standing still.

Strange old man and crazy,
  Shall we forces join?
Will you grind your organ
  To these songs of mine?

August Graf von Platen

The Pilgrim before St. Just

'Tis night and storms sweep by and loudly roar,
Hispanian monks, unlock to me your door.

Till matin bell awakes, here let me stay,
Which frightens you to prayers and church away.

Prepare for me all that your House can do,
Your robe of Order and a coffin too.

Grudge me not one small cell, and consecrate
Me, to whom half the world belonged of late.

This head, which stoops beneath the scissors now,
Has worn full many a crown upon its brow.

Imperial ermine decked with princely state,
Those shoulders which are clad with cowl sedate.

Now am I like the dead before I'm cold,
And fall to ruins like the empire old.

A Winter Sigh

The heavens above laugh bright and blue,
Ah, would that the earth were green!
The winds cut keen—ah, that soft they blew,
The snow doth glitter, ah, were it dew,
Ah, would that the earth were green!

Winter Song

Patience, thou small bud, shrinking
    Beneath the cold spring moon;
As yet 'tis all too early,
    As yet 'tis all too soon.

To-day I pass and leave thee,
    Marking thy wood retreat,
But when the spring returneth,
    I'll come and fetch thee, sweet.

Lot of the Lyrist

Ever cleaves our soul unto action. Matter
Is the mighty pulse of the world, and therefore
Mostly chants to ears that are deaf, the exalted
    Lyrical Poet.

Platen

To each grasp doth readily Homer lend him,
Spreading out his tissue of gorgeous fable;
Whilst with ease the Dramatist gains the people's
    Rapturous plaudits.

But thy flight, oh, Pindar, thy art, oh, Flaccus,
But thy weighty pondering word, oh, Petrarch,
Doth impress more slowly our hearts; the masses
    Ne'er understand it.

Theirs but inner charm, not the careless measure
Of some love lay lilted to please proud beauty;
For no heedless glance may e'er scan their genius'
    Lofty sublimeness.

Ever seems familiar their name, resounding
Full within the ear of mankind. Yet seldom
Are they joined in homage and friendship by some
    Spirit congenial.

Annette von Droste-Hülshof

The Boy on the Moor

Oh, drear is the way o'er the moor by night,
When the swamp-bred mists are flying,
When the fog-wreaths whirl like phantoms light,
When the bramble clasps the thorn-bush tight,
When at every footstep a clear rill springs,
And from out each crevice it oozes and sings;
Oh, drear is the way o'er the moor by night
When the reeds in the wind are sighing.

Close pressing his books runs the trembling boy,
His speed by terror heightened;
The wind moans past with hollow sigh—
What rustles in yonder bush close by?
'Tis the spectre gravedigger, appearing again,
Who stole the best peat and squandered the gain;—
He breaks through the boughs like stray cattle—he's nigh!—
Down shrinks the boy, sore frightened.

Droste-Hülshof

From the shore the stunted willows loom,
The firs are uncannily bending,
The boy speeds on through the tangled broom,
Through giant rushes, like spears in the gloom;
Hark, how it rustles and crackles loud!
'Tis the haunted spinner-girl, lazy and proud,
'Tis the ghostly Jenny, whose wretched doom
To twirl her spindle unending.

On, on, he flies, through brake and bush,
O'er moorland flat and hilly,
From under his footsteps oozes the slush
Like a melody weird from sedge and rush;
That is the pilfering fiddler, Joe,
Who stole the wedding presents, you know,—
You can hear him plainly now, oh hush!
His fiddle squeaking shrilly.

The ground splits open with yell and groan,
Her spectral arms wild tosses
The phantom Margaret and makes her moan:
"Oh, my lost soul, ochone! ochone!"—
The boy darts on like a frightened deer,
Were not his guardian angel near,
One day were found his bleaching bone
'Neath moorland peats and mosses.

At length the ground grows firm, and bright
A lamp by the willow yonder

Doth shed a safe and homely light;
The boy still trembles with dread and fright;
He pauses, hard breathing, and back askance
O'er his shoulder he throws a shy wild glance:—
Oh, the haunted heath was eerie by night,
'Twas dread o'er the moor to wander.

The Deserted House

A HOUSE stands empty down the glen,
For years ago has died the keeper;
And there I rest me now and then,
Half buried beneath brush and creeper;
A wilderness, wherein the day
But half uplifts his eyelid weary;—
The rocky gap glooms dark and dreary,
O'ershadowed by gaunt branches gray.

I listen dreamily the flies'
Soft drowsy hum as they flash o'er me,
The forest echoes as with sighs,
Stray beetles blindly drone before me;
And when the sunset fires imbue
These rocks that ooze with wet down creeping,
Then, as an eye that has been weeping,
They seem all red and dull of hue.

Droste-Hülshof

Where by yon arbour's rank decay
Wild shoots are growing, thin and weedy,
Carnation slips now even stray
O'er marshy places, wet and reedy;
The rock-drip sets in pools of slush,
That steal, without or aim or order,
Lazily round the old box border
And soak in by the fennel bush.

The thatch, with moss encrusted green,
Is overgrown with tangled litter,
And in the broken pane is seen
A spider's web strangely a-glitter;
For, see, like leaf of golden brown,
A wing of dragon-fly hangs pendent,
While its cuirass' shield resplendent,
Headless, doth dangle lower down.

Sometimes a butterfly has strayed
Into the glen at noontide hour,
And for a second it has played
Round the narcissus' sickly flower;—
When o'er the chasm it doth fly,
Its croon the pigeon wild is hushing,
You only hear its pinions rushing
And see its shadow flitting by.

And on the hearthstone, where the snow
For years down the wide flue has sifted,

Gray mildew rankly doth o'ergrow
The ashes that lie dank and drifted;
Some strands of tangled yarn still rest,
Hanging from roof on staple rusty,
Almost like hair, matted and musty,
And in it, lo! a last year's nest.

And from the rafters overhead
Swings a dog's collar, old and dusty,
Whereon " Diana " may be read,
Broidered in worsteds coarse and rusty;
That pipe, too, surely was forgot,
When they nailed down the coffin's cover,—
The man was buried—and that over
The poor old faithful dog was shot.

As I sit idly thus and dream,
I hear the field-mouse stealthy gnawing,
The squirrel barks its sharp short scream,
Softened resounds the rooks' far cawing;
And then I sometimes feel a chill,
As though I heard them starting gladly
Upon their rounds,—Di barking madly,
And the dead keeper whistling still.

Heinrich Heine

Du bist wie eine Blume

E'EN as a lovely flower,
    So fair, so pure, thou art ;
I gaze on thee, and sadness
    Comes stealing o'er my heart.

My hands I fain had folded
    Upon thy soft brown hair,
Praying that God may keep thee
    So lovely, pure and fair.

Wie der Mond sich leuchtend dränget

As the moon bursts forth in splendour
    From the clouds that gloom it o'er,
Thus there starts a radiant vision
    Forth from troubled times of yore.

On the deck again we're sitting,
   Down the Rhine we proudly flow,
And the deep rich banks of summer
   In the evening sunset glow.

At my lady's feet reclining,
   Pondering dreamily I lay;
O'er her pale beloved features
   Golden-threaded sunbeams play.

Music ringing, children singing,
   Strange sweet joy on every side!
Deeper grew the vault of heaven,
   And the soul expanded wide.

Fairy-like each passed before us,
   Mountain, wood, and castle high;
And I saw it all reflected
   In my lady's beauteous eye.

Was will die einsame Thräne

WHAT means this lonely teardrop,
   It only dims mine eye;
'Twas left behind, remaining,
   From times long since gone by.

It had many shining sisters,
   That all have passed away,
Away with my joy and my sorrow
   In night and storm fled away.

Like mist, too, have departed
   Those blue stars sweet and bright,
That smiled such joy and sorrow
   Into my heart's lone night.

My love itself has faded,
   E'en like an idle breath;
Thou solitary teardrop,
   Dissolve thou, too, in death.

Ich stand in dunkeln Träumen

I GAZED upon her picture,
   My bosom dark with strife,
And her beloved features
   Kindled to secret life.

Around her lips there trembled
   A smile so sweet, so dear,
While drops of heavenly sadness
   Within her eyes shone clear.

And mine were also streaming
   With teardrops wild and wet—
And oh, I cannot believe it,
   That I have lost you yet !

Wir sassen am Fischerhause

WE sat at the fisherman's cottage,
   And gazed upon the sea ;
Then came the mists of evening,
   And rose up silently.

The lights within the lighthouse
   Were kindled one by one,
We saw still a ship in the distance
   On the dim horizon alone.

We spoke of tempest and shipwreck,
   Of sailors and of their life,
And how 'twixt clouds and billows
   They're tossed, 'twixt joy and strife.

We spoke of distant countries
   From North to South that range,
Of strange phantastic nations,
   And their customs quaint and strange.

Heine

The Ganges is flooded with splendour,
    And perfumes waft through the air,
And gentle people are kneeling
    To Lotos flowers fair.

In Lapland the people are dirty,
    Flat-headed, large-mouthed, and small;
They squat round the fire, and frying
    Their fish, they shout and they squall.

The girls all gravely listened,
    No word was spoken at last;
The ship we could see no longer,
    Darkness was settling so fast.

Wie kannst du ruhig schlafen

How canst thou sleep so softly,
    Knowing I am alive?
My old hot wrath returneth,
    And then my bondage I rive.

Dost know the old, old legend:
    How once a lover dead
Fetched down to the grave his sweetheart,
    At the hour of midnight dread?

Fairest of maids, believe me,
    Thou sweetest, too, by far :
I am alive, and stronger
    Than any dead men are !

Am Kreuzweg ward begraben

AT the cross-roads he lies buried
    Who ended his life in shame ;
And there grows a pale blue flower,
    The Felon's Flower by name.

At the cross-roads I stood sighing,
    Silent the night and drear ;
All gently swayed the flower
    In the moonlight cold and clear.

Deine weissen Lilienfinger

YOUR white, slender lily fingers,
Oh, if I once more could kiss them,
And could press them to my heart,
And then swoon in silent weeping.

Your clear violet eyes are ever,
Ever present, day and night ;
What may mean, I ask for ever,
What may mean those sweet blue riddles?

Heine

Das gelbe Laub erzittert

Down fall and flutter sadly
    The yellow leaves and sere,—
And all that is fair and lovely
    Fades, trembling, to the bier.

The forest is steeped in the splendour
    Of a sad and sorrowful light ;
Perchance, these are the last kisses
    Of summer, departing bright.

And my hot tears upwelling,
    Gush from my inmost heart,
As I think of that hour when sadly
    We two did kiss and part.

I had to leave you, my darling,
    Knowing you soon must die !
You were the fading forest,
    Departing summer I !

Am leuchtenden Sommermorgen

Around the garden I wander
    On this radiant summer morn,
The flowers are whispering together,
    But I am all sad and forlorn.

The flowers are whispering together,
  With pity my face they scan :
" Be not angry with our sister,
  Thou sad and pale-faced man."

Die Mitternacht war kalt und stumm

THE midnight hour was dreary and cold,
Loud wailing I strayed through wood and wold.
From their sleep I shook in despairing passion
The trees—they shook their heads in compassion.

The Message

UP, boy ! Arise and saddle quick,
  And mount your swiftest steed,
And to King Duncan's castle ride
  O'er bush and brake with speed.

There slip into the stable soft,
  Till one shall see you hide,
Then ask him : Which of Duncan's girls
  Is she that is a bride ?

And if he say : The dark-haired one,
  Then give your mare the spur ;
But if he say : The fair-haired one,
  You need not hurry her.

You only need, if that's the case,
   Buy me a hempen cord,
Ride slowly back and give it me,
   But never speak a word.

Dämmernd liegt der Sommerabend

DIMLY sinks the summer evening
Over wood and over meadow;
And the golden moon shines radiant,
Balm diffusing, from the azure.

By the brook sings loud the cricket,
And the water clear is troubled,
And you hear a gentle plashing,
A soft breathing through the stillness.

By the brook, alone, see yonder,
Where doth bathe the lovely Nixie;
Arms and bosom, white and dazzling,
Gleaming in the moon's pale silver.

Nacht liegt auf den fremden Wegen

NIGHT lies on the silent highways,
   Sick my heart, my limbs how weary;
Then like gentle balm descendeth,
   Moon, thy soft light on me dreary.

Gentle moon, all dread nocturnal
   With thy sweet light thou dost banish;
And mine eyes with tears well over,
   And my torments melt and vanish.

Almansor

I.

IN Cordova's old cathedral
Thirteen hundred columns tower;
Thirteen hundred giant columns
Bear the cupola stupendous.

And on walls and domes and pillars,
Run in quaint design and tracery,
From the roof unto the basement,
Passages from out the Koran.

Moorish monarchs whilom builded
This cathedral unto Allah
And his praise, but much has altered
In the vortex dark of ages.

On the tower where the warden
Called to prayer the Moslem Faithful,
Now the melancholy droning
Hum of Christian bells is ringing.

On the steps where the Believers
Sung the praises of the Prophet,
Now sleek tonsured priests are showing
Their stale mass's mawkish marvel.

Lo, they wriggle and they posture
'Fore their painted gaudy puppets;
Incense, tinkling, quack, and gabble,
And the silly tapers twinkle.

In Cordova's old cathedral
Stands Almansor ben Abdullah,
Silent looks he on the pillars,
And these secret words he mutters:

"Oh, ye columns, strong and mighty,
Once adorned in praise of Allah!
Serving, ye must now do homage
To the Christian faith detested.

"If you're so accommodating,
And you bear your load in patience,
Why, the weaker one must surely
Likewise know how to conform him."

And behold, with smiling features,
Doth Almansor ben Abdullah,
O'er the font embellished bend him,
In Cordova's old cathedral.

II.

Hastily he leaves the transept,
Sweeps away on his wild charger,
And his wet locks in the breezes,
And his hat's black plumes are flying.

On the way to Alkolea,
All along the Guadalquivir,
Where the almonds white are blowing,
And the orange, rich and yellow ;

There doth ride the knight full cheerly,
Whistling, singing, laughing gaily,
And the birds around join chorus,
With the river's many waters.

In the halls of Alkolea,
Dwelleth Clara of Alveras,
In Navarre fights now her father,
And from less restraint she suffers.

From afar doth hear Almansor
Kettledrum and trumpet braying,
And he sees the castle's torches
Flashing through the forest shadows.

In the halls of Alkolea
Dance twelve ladies, bright and beauteous,
Dance twelve handsome knights and gallant—
Best of all Almansor dances.

As though winged by buoyant spirits
He around the room doth flutter,
And with words of sweetest flatt'ry
He doth whisper every lady.

The fair hands of Isabella
He doth kiss, away quick darting;
Then sits down before Elvira,
In her face with rapture gazing.

Laughing, he asks Leonora,
Whether he to-day doth please her?
And he shows the golden crosses
Newly broidered in his mantle.

Lastly, he assures each lady
In his heart her image liveth:
And, "as true as I'm a Christian,'
Swears he thirty times that evening.

III.

In the halls of Alkolea
Jest and laughter now are silent,
Vanished are the lords and ladies,
And the lights are all extinguished.

Donna Clara and Almansor
Are alone in the wide chamber;
Lonely sheds the last dim taper
On the twain its mournful radiance.

On the settle sits the lady,
On a stool the knight before her,
And his head, with slumber heavy,
Rests upon her knees belovèd.

Oil of roses from gold flasket,
Pours the lady, fond and anxious,
On the dark locks of Almansor—
And, behold, he sigheth deeply.

Sweetest kiss, with lips so tender,
Breathes the lady, fond and anxious,
On the dark locks of Almansor—
And, behold, his brow clouds over.

Brightest shower, from eyes so shining,
Weeps the lady, fond and anxious,
On the dark locks of Almansor—
And, behold, his lips they quiver.

And he dreams : again he standeth,
With bowed head, all wet and dripping,
In Cordova's old cathedral,
And he hears dark voices many.

All the lofty giant columns
He hears muttering, grimly wrathful,
That they will not bear it longer,—
And they tremble and they totter ;—

And they fiercely crack and crumble;
Pale as death grow priest and people;
With wild crash the dome o'erwhelmeth,
And the Christian gods are wailing.

Leise zieht durch mein Gemüth

Soft and gently through my soul
   Sweetest bells are ringing;
Speed you forth, my little song,
   Of spring-time gaily singing!

Speed you onward to a house
   Where sweet flowers are fleeting!
If, perchance, a rose you see,
   Say, I send her greeting!

Der Schmetterling ist in die Rose verliebt

The butterfly is in love with the rose,
   And hovers around her alway;
But a golden sunbeam loves him again,
   And flutters around him all day.

But tell me with whom is the rose in love?
   That would I know sooner by far;
Or is it the singing nightingale,
   Or the silent evening star?

I know not with whom is the rose in love;
  But I love you all as ye are:
The butterfly, sunbeam, and nightingale,
  The rose, and the evening star.

Es war ein alter Koenig

Was once an ancient monarch,
Heavy his heart, his locks were gray;
This poor and aged monarch
Took a wife so young and gay.

Was once a page-boy handsome,
With lightsome heart and curly hair;
The silken train he carried
Of the Queen so young and fair.

Dost know the old old story?
It sounds so sweet, so sad to tell—
Both were obliged to perish,
They loved each other too well.

Mit schwarzen Segeln segelt mein Schiff

With gloomy sails my ship doth fly
  Far over the stormy main;
You know how woe of heart I am,
  And yet you cause my pain.

Heine

Your heart is faithless as the wind,
    Veering like any vane ;
With gloomy sails my ship doth fly
    Far over the stormy main.

Clarissa

"Es kommt zu spät was Du mir lächelst"

Too late come now your smiles of promise,
    Alas! they come too late, your sighs!
Long time has died the love within me
    You cruelly once did despise.

Too late comes now your love and tardy!
    And all your ardent glances fall
Upon a heart, cold, irresponsive,
    Like sunshine on a grave withal.

   *   *   *   *

One thing I'd know: when we have perished,
    Where is it that our soul doth go?
Where is the fire that is extinguished?
    Where is the wind but now did blow?

Katharine

"Ein schoener Stern geht auf in meiner Nacht"

A STAR dawns beauteous in my gloomy night,
A star, that sheds sweet comfort with its light,
Promising me new life and joy,—
    Ah, do not lie!

Like as the ocean to the moon swells free,
So mounts my soul, daring and glad to thee,
To thee, and to thy light of joy,—
    Ah, do not lie!

Desist

The day with night is in love,
And spring is in love with winter,
Life is enamoured of death,—
And thou, thou lovest me!

Thou lovest me—already dread
And gruesome shadows seize thee,
All thy fresh beauty fades,
To death thy soul is bleeding.

Desist from me, and only love
The butterflies that flutter
Careless and lightsome in the sun,—
Desist from me and from ruin.

Heinrich

In the courtyard of Canossa
Stands the German Emperor Heinrich,
Barefoot and in shirt of penance,
And the night is cold and rainy.

Peering from an upper window
Twain look down, while glints the moonlight
On the bald pate of Gregorius
And the white breasts of Mathildis.

Heinrich he, with lips all pallid,
Murmurs pious paternosters,
But within his heart of emperor,
Secretly he chafes and gnashes:

"Far off, in my German country,
Rise those strong and sturdy mountains,
And in shafts so still and silent,
Grows the iron for a war-axe.

"Far off, in my German country,
Rustle mighty oaken forests,
And within the tallest oak stems
Grows the wood for this same war-axe.

"Thou, my loved and trusty country,
Thou, too, shall bring forth the champion
Who shall smite down with his war-axe
Yonder serpent of my torments."

Mittelalterliche Roheit

RUDE mediæval barbarism
To fine arts is slowly yielding;
Chief machine of modern culture
Is undoubtedly the piano.

Railways, too, a wholesome influence
Exercise on home life, surely,
For they render it so easy
From one's family to fly.

What a pity that my spinal
Illness renders it unlikely
That I shall remain much longer
In this fast progressive world?

THE NORTH SEA
First Part
Coronation

O songs! ye my good songs!
Arise, your armour don!
Let the trumpet sound forth,
And raise me on shield
This fair young maiden,
Who now shall reign over
My whole heart as Queen!
Hail to thee, O thou fair young Queen!

From the sun up above
I will tear out the dazzling red gold,
And will weave therefrom a diadem
For thy consecrated head;
From the fluttering blue silken tent of heaven,
Wherein flash the diamonds of night,
I will cut thee a costly garment,
And will hang it as royal mantle
Around thy regal shoulders.

I will give thee a court-state
Of primly bedight sonnets,

Of haughty terzines and of courtly stanzas;
My wit shall attend thee as footman,
As jester my imagination,
While as herald, the tearful smile in escutcheon,
My humour shall serve thee.
But myself, O Queen,
Will kneel down before thee,
And present to thee on purple velvet—
In deepest homage,
The little sense
Which thy fair predecessor
In mercy hath left me.

Twilight

By the dim sea-shore
Lonely I sat, and thought-afflicted.
The sun sank low, and sinking he shed
Rose and vermilion upon the waters,
And the white foaming waves,
Urged on by the tide,
Foamed and murmured yet nearer and nearer—
A curious jumble of whispering and wailing,
Of soft rippling laughter and sobbing and sighing,
And in between all a low lullaby singing.
Methought I heard ancient forgotten legends
And world-old sweet stories,
Which once as a boy

Heine

I heard from my playmates,
When, of a summer's evening,
We crouched down to tell stories
On the stones of the doorstep,
With small listening hearts,
And bright curious eyes ;
While the big grown-up girls
Were sitting opposite
At flowery and fragrant windows,
Their rosy faces
Smiling and moonshine-illumined.

Sunset

THE red and glowing sun descends
Into the silver-gray shuddering ocean,
That ripples and heaves from its depth to receive it ;
Airy images, tenderly flushed,
Glide gently after ; while just opposite
From autumnly drift of sad dim clouds
Breaks forth the moon,
A pale face and deathlike ;
Behind her, as tiny sparks, the stars
Glimmer faintly through nebulous space.

   Once united in the high heavens,
Beamed in conjugal radiance
Luna, the goddess, and Sol, the god,

And round them clustered the stars,
Their little innocent children.
But sland'rous tongues whispered discord and evil,
And the bright and exalted couple
Parted in anger.

Now in the day-time, in lonely glory,
Parades on high the God of the Sun,
Adored and much lauded
For his fierce splendour,
By proud men, hardened by fortune.
But in the night
Luna moves o'er the sky,
The forsaken mother,
With her starry band of orphan children,
And she beams with soft melancholy,
And loving maidens and gentle poets
Offer her tears and ditties.

Poor tender Luna! Womanlike loves she,
Loves without ceasing her handsome husband;
And, towards evening, all trembling and pale,
You see her peering from fleecy clouds,
And gazing with aching heart
On the Departing; and fain would she cry
Anxiously: "Come!
Come, the children are calling for you—"
But the Sun-god, proud and obdurate,
At sight of his wife,

Flushes a yet deeper purple
With anger and grief,
And unrelenting he hastens down
To his cold and watery widower's bed.

  * * * *

Evil and slanderous tongues
Thus brought pain and disaster,
Even on immortal gods;
And the wretched gods, high up in the heavens,
Pursue in anguish
And endless despair
Their dreary course,
And cannot die,
And ever drag with them
Their radiant sorrow.

But I, a man only,
Lowly born and death-favoured,
Complain no longer.

The Night on the Beach

STARLESS and cold is the night;
Old Ocean yawns,
And flat on the ocean, upon his belly,
Squats the uncouth North Wind;
And stealthily croaking, with groan and with grunt,
Like a crotchety grumbler waxing good-humoured,

He babbles into the waters
Mad tales without number;
Tales of giants, breathing of slaughter,
And world-old stories of Norway;
And ever between he laughs, and howls out
Incantations from Edda
And ancient Runes,
So darkly defiant and potent of spell
That the white ocean children
Leap up high and exulting
In turbulent frenzy.

   Meanwhile, on the flat lone shore,
O'er the tide-washed sands,
Strides a stranger whose throbbing heart
Beats yet wilder than wind and waves.
Whither he treads
Sparks fly, and shells crunch beneath him;
And he wraps him up in his sombre mantle,
And strides on fast through the wind and the night,
Safely led by the glimmering taper,
That beckons so sweetly inviting
From the fisherman's lonely cottage.

   Father and brothers are out at sea,
And all alone by herself was left
In the cottage the fisherman's daughter,
The wondrously beautiful fisherman's daughter.
By the hearth sits she,

And lists to the kettle's
Drowsy song, full of sweet promise;
Fuel and sticks she adds to the fire,
And blows thereon,
And the flickering red light
As by magic illumines
Her blooming features,
And her tender white shoulder
That peeps forth pathetic
From coarse linen kirtle,
And illumines, too, her small hand,
Carefully tying yet faster her garments
Round her slender waist.

But on a sudden the door springs open,
And there enters the stranger nocturnal;
Full and assured of love
Rests his eye on the fair slight maiden,
Who trembles before him
Like unto a frightened lily;
And he throws his cloak on the ground,
Aud he laughs and says:
"Look you, my child, I have kept my word,
And I come, and there comes
Unto me the old time
When the gods descended from heaven
Unto the daughters of men,
And embraced the daughters of men,
And begat with them

Sceptre-bearing races of Kings,
And Heroes, world-renowned.
But stand not amazed, my child, any longer
At my divinity,
But give me some tea with hot rum, I beseech you,
For it's cold outside,
And on such a raw night
Even we shiver, we gods eternal,
And easily catch we most heavenly colds,
And coughs divinely immortal."

Poseidon

THE sunbeams were playing
Lightly over the billowy ocean;
Far out at sea I saw shining the ship
That was to bear me homewards;
But the right wind as yet was wanting,
And tranquilly on the white sands I was sitting
By the lonely sea,
And I read the song of Ulysses,
That old, that ever youthful song,
From whose ocean-murmuring leaves
Rose joyfully
The breath of the gods,
And the sunny spring of mankind,
And the cloudless sky of fair Hellas.

Heine

My noble and faithful heart accompanied
The son of Laertes in toil and disaster:
It sat down with him, grieving in spirit,
At kindly hearths,
Where queens sat spinning deep rich purple;
It helped him to lie and to escape deftly
From giants' caves and from nymphs' white arms;
It followed him into Kimmerian night.
Through storm and through shipwreck,
And suffered with him unspeakable anguish.

Sighing said I, " Revengeful Poseidon,
Thy anger is awful,
And myself am afraid
Of my own return home."

Scarcely had I spoken the words,
When the sea foamed up high,
And from the white-crested billows arose
The head of the god, crowned with sea-weed,
And cried he, contemptuous:

" Fear not, my dear little Poet!
I've no intention to harm in the least
Thy poor little bark,
Nor frighten thee out of thy poor little wits
With too boist'rous a rocking:
For thou, little Poet, hast never incensed me,
Thou never hast shaken the smallest turret

Of the holy city of Priam;
Nor hast thou singed e'en a single hair
From the eye of my son Polyphemus;
And never as yet has the Goddess of Wisdom,
Pallas Athenæ, stood counselling beside thee."

   Thus cried out Poseidon,
And dived back into the ocean;
And at the vulgar old sailor's joke
I heard Amphitrite, the coarse fish-woman,
And the silly daughters of Nereus,
Giggling beneath the waters.

Declaration

THE evening shadows fell dim and sad,
Roughly the tide tumbled in,
And I sat on the beach and gazed
On the white dance of waters;
And yearning, I felt a deep wistful longing
For thee, thou dear Image,
That followest me ever,
And callest me ever,
Always and ever,
In the blast of the wind, in the roar of the sea,
In the sighing of my own heart.

With slender reed I wrote on the sand:
"Agnes! I love you!"
But unkind waves crept up and washed over
The sweet confession
And blotted it out.
Thou brittle reed, thou wild-whirling sand,
Ye dissolving billows, I trust ye no longer!
The sky grows darker, my heart throbs wilder,
And with strong hand, from the forests of Norway,
I tear out the loftiest pine;
And I dip it into
The red-hot glowing crater of Etna,
And with this fiery pen and gigantic
I write on the dark vault of heaven:
"Agnes! I love you!"

Thus every night, blazing shall flare
On high my eternal letters of flame,
And all generations to come hereafter
Shall read, exulting, the rapturous words:
"Agnes! I love you!"

At Night in the Cabin

Its pearls doth have the ocean,
And heaven hath its stars,
But oh, my heart, my heart,
My heart doth have its love.

Large is the ocean and heaven,
    But larger is my own heart,
And fairer than pearls and stars
    Flashes and beams my love.

Thou young, thou sweet young maiden,
    Come to my swelling heart;
My heart, the sea, and the heavens,
    Are melting for very love.

    *   *   *   *

Fain I'd press my lips in anguish,
Wildly press them, wildly weeping,
On the dark blue vault of heaven,
Where the bright-eyed stars are shining.

For yon stars so brightly shining
Are the eyes of my Beloved,
And a thousandfold they greet me
From the dark blue vault of heaven.

To the dark blue vault of heaven,
To the eyes of my Beloved,
Both my hands I lift devoutly,
And I pray, and I petition:

"Beauteous eyes, ye gracious tapers,
Consecrate my soul and bless it;
Let me die, and thus acquire
You and all the heaven within you!"

    *   *   *   *

Heine

From those heavenly eyes above me
Golden sparks fall trembling downwards,
And my soul expands with longing,
Evermore with love and longing.

Oh, ye heavenly eyes above me,
Inundate my soul with weeping,
That my spirit may run over
With the bright and starry shower.

* * * *

Lulled to rest by ocean billows,
And by dreamy thoughts that wander,
Calm I lie within the cabin,
In the dark berth in the corner.

Through the open porthole gazing,
Bright I see the stars above me,
Those belovèd eyes and tender
Of my sweet and Well-Beloved.

Those belovèd eyes and tender
Brightly watch and guard my pillow,
And they glimmer and they shimmer
In the dark blue vault of heaven.

Towards the dark blue vault of heaven
Rapt I gaze for many an hour,
Till a silver veil of sea-mist,
Envious, hides those dear eyes from me.

* * * *

Against the wooden planking
Where lies my dreaming head,
Dash the billows, the boisterous billows;
They ripple and murmur,
Softly whispering mine ear:
" Deluded fool!
Your arm is short, and the heavens are far off,
And the stars up above are riveted fast
With golden nails,—
Idle yearning and idle sighing,
'Twere best for you to go to sleep."

   * * * *

In dreams I saw a plain immense and dreary,
 Deep covered o'er with silent driven snow;
And underneath the snow myself lay buried,
 And slept the cold and lonely sleep of death.

But from the dark blue heavens above down-gleaming
 Upon my grave, the starry eyes were shining,
Those tender eyes! And lo, they beam in triumph
 And gladness calm, and, too, in Love unbounded.

Storm

Fierce rages the storm,
And it lashes the waves,
And the waves, wild furious and boiling,
Tower tumultuous, white water-mountains,

Heaving with angry life;
And the frail bark climbs them
With arduous haste,
And sudden it dashes deep down
Into black and cavernous abysses of billows.

   O Sea!
Mother of Beauty, the foam-born Goddess!
Grandmother of Love! I pray you to spare me!
Already hovers o'erhead, scenting corpses,
The ghostly white sea-mew,
And whets on the mast her cruel beak,
And eagerly lusts for the heart
Which rings of the praise of thy daughter,
And which thy grandson, the little rogue,
Has chosen as plaything.

   In vain my entreaties and prayers!
My cry dies away in the rushing storm,
In the battle-cry of the winds.
They bluster and pipe and bellow and roar,
Like a Madhouse of Sound!
And, in between, I distinctly can hear
Siren harp-strains,
And yearning wild song;
Song soul-melting and song soul-rending,
And I recognize, too, the voice.

   Far away, on the rocky coast of Scotland,
A grey old castle boldly juts out

Over the boiling tide;
There, by a vaulted oriel window
Stands a beautiful woman,
Fragile and delicate, pale as death.
And she strikes her harp and sings,
And the storm dishevels her long wild tresses,
And bears away her gloomy song
Far over the raging waste of waters.

Ocean Calm

DEEP repose lies on the ocean,
And the sun sheds down his radiance;
Through the flashing waves like jewels
Draws the ship her emerald furrows.

Near the wheel doth lie the boatswain,
Sleeping sweetly, snoring softly;
By the masts sits, tarred and spattered,
Mending sails, the cabin boy.

From his cheeks, begrimed and dirty,
Flashes forth a tell-tale scarlet,
Sadly his wide mouth is quivering,
And his fine eyes have been weeping.

For the captain stands before him,
Scolding, railing, swearing roundly:

"Greedy pilferer! thou hast basely
Stolen a herring from my barrel!"

Calm the ocean! from the billows
Leaps a merry little spratling,
Warms its small head in the sunshine,
Whisks its little tail so frisky.

But a gull from out its eyry
Darts upon that frisky spratling,
And her rapid prey fast seizing,
Soars again into the azure.

Sea-Vision

But I lay at the edge of the vessel,
And gazed with eye that was dreaming
Down into the clear crystal water,
And gazed down deeper and deeper
Till far on the ground of the ocean,
At first like mists of twilight,
But soon more defined in colour and substance.
Domes of churches appeared and steeples,
And at length, clear as day, an entire town;
Antiquated, Netherlandish,
And thronged with people.
Solemn men, draped in black mantles,
With snowy neck ruffs and chains of honour,

With rapiers long, and eke long faces,
Soberly cross the swarming market
To the Town-hall, ascended by lofty steps,
Where Imperial statues of stone
Guard entrance with sceptre and sword.
Not far off, before long row of houses,
Where lindens, cut into shapes fantastic,
Are mirrored in glittering windows,
Maidens walk in rustling silk garments,—
Slim young girls, their fresh flower-faces
Demurely inclosed by modest black coifs,
And waving tresses of gold;
Gay young fellows, in Spanish costume,
Swagger by, haughtily nodding;
Aged women,
In brown old-fashioned dresses,
Carrying rosaries and prayer-books,
Hasten with faltering steps
To the great Cathedral,
Urged on by the peal of the organ,
And by the clanging of bells.

 Myself am moved by the secret
Mysterious power of the distant strain:
An infinite yearning, a sorrow profound
Steals o'er my heart,
My scarcely healed heart;—
I feel as though its wounds were kissed open
Once more by beloved lips,

And that again they were bleeding
Red warm drops of blood,
Which trickle down slow and slowly
Upon an old mansion below
In the deep ocean city;
Upon a dreary old gabled mansion,
That stands in sad drear solitude,
Save that at a lower window
A girl is sitting,
Leaning her head on her hand,
Like a poor and forgotten child—
And I know thee, thou poor and forgotten child!

So deep then, even as deep as ocean,
Didst thou hide from me
In childish caprice,
And couldst return again never,
And sattest, a stranger among strange people,
For centuries!
The while I, with sorrowing soul,
The wide world over have sought thee,
Aye, without ceasing have sought thee,
Thou ever loved one,
Oh, thou long lost one,
At last found again!
And now I have found thee, again I behold
Thy sweet fair face,
And those grave earnest eyes,
And the dear old smile—

And never, never again will I leave thee,
And I am coming to thee,
And with open arms
Let me sink to thy heart——

   But just in the nick of time
The Captain seized hold of my foot,
And pulled me away from the edge of the vessel,
And cried, vexatiously laughing :
" What the deuce, my dear sir, are you up to ? "

Cleansing

STAY thou below in thy ocean depths,
Delirious Dream,
That once, ah, many a night,
Hast tormented my heart with false happiness,
And to-day, as Sea Phantom
Doth threaten me even in broad daylight !—
Stay thou below, for ever and ever,
And I will throw down to thee still
All my anguish and sin,
And the foolscap of folly
Which has jingled long time round my head;
And the cold glittering snake-skin
Of hypocrisy,
Which was coiled long time round my soul,

Heine

My poisoned soul,
My God-denying, angel-denying,
Most wretched soul !
Yoho ! yoho ! Here comes the wind !
Hoist up the sails ! they flap and they swell !
O'er the calmly-fatal expanse
The good ship flies,
And, delivered, the Soul shouts exulting.

Peace

THE sun stood high in the heavens,
White-robed in masses of cloud ;
The ocean was calm,
And musing I lay by the helm of the vessel,
Dreamily pondering,—and half in waking
And half in sleeping, Christ I beheld,
The world's Redeemer ;
In white waving vesture,
He strode, a giant form,
Over land and sea ;
His head touched unto the heavens,
His hands He stretched out, blessing,
Over land and sea :
And lo, as heart in His breast
He carried the sun,
The red flaming sun ;

And the red flaming Sun-Heart
Poured its tender beams of grace,
Illuming and warming,
Over land and sea.

Pealing bells rang clearly and sweetly,
Drawing, as with garlands of roses,
Drawing, swanlike, the gliding ship
Lightly, playfully to the green shore,
Where men are living in yon high-towered
And steepled city.

Oh, wonder of Peace ! How hushed the town !
The jarring din of noisy tradescrafts
Has ceased in stifling buildings and shops ;
And through the clean echoing streets
Wander people all clad in white,
And bearing branches of palm ;
And where two meet,
They gaze on each other in brotherly kindness
And trembling with love and with sweet resignation,
Each kisses each on the brow ;
And they lift up their eyes
To the Saviour's Sun-Heart,
That flashes down in glad atonement
Its precious blood ;
And thrice blessed they say :
Praised be Jesus Christ."

SECOND PART

Good-Morrow

THALATTA! Thalatta!
Hail to thee, thou eternal sea!
Hail to thee, ten thousand times, hail!
With rejoicing heart
I bid thee welcome,
As once, long ago, did welcome thee
Ten thousand Greek hearts,
Hardship-battling, homesick-yearning,
World-renowned Greek hearts.

The billows surged,
They foamed and murmured,
The sun poured down, as in haste,
Flickering ripples of rosy light;
Long strings of frightened seagulls
Flutter away shrill screaming;
War-horses trample, and shields clash loudly,
And far resounds the triumphant cry:
Thalatta! Thalatta!

Hail to thee, thou eternal sea!
Like accents of home thy waters are whispering,
And dreams of childhood lustrous I see
Through thy limpid and crystalline wave;

Calling to mind the dear old memories
Of dear and delightful toys,
Of all the glittering Christmas presents,
Of all the red-branched forests of coral,
The pearls, the goldfish and bright-coloured shells,
Which thou dost hide mysteriously
Deep down in thy clear house of crystal.

   Oh, how have I languished in dreary exile!
Like unto a withered flower
In the botanist's capsule of tin,
My heart lay dead in my breast.
Methought I was prisoned a long sad winter,
A sick man kept in a darkened chamber;
And now I suddenly leave it,
And outside meets me the dazzling Spring,
Tenderly verdant and sun-awakened;
And rustling trees shed snowy petals,
And tender young flowers gaze on me
With their bright fragrant eyes;
And the air is full of laughter and gladness,
And rich with the breath of blossoms,
And in the blue sky the birds are singing—
Thalatta! Thalatta!

   Oh, my brave Anabasis-heart!
How often, ah! how sadly often
Wast thou pressed hard by the North's fair Barbarians!
From large and conquering eyes

They shot forth burning arrows;
With crooked words as sharp as a rapier
They threatened to pierce my bosom;
With cuneiform angular missives they battered
My poor stunned brains;
In vain I held out my shield for protection,
The arrows hissed and the blows rained down,
And hard pressed I was pushed to the sea
By the North's fair Barbarians,—
And breathing freely, I greet the sea,
The sea my deliverer, the sea my friend,
Thalatta! Thalatta!

The Thunderstorm

Lurid the thunderstorm lies on the ocean,
And through the banks of black cloud
Flashes the red-forked lightning,
Swift blazing forth and as swift disappearing.
Like wit from the head of Kronion.
Over the drearily restless waters
Solemnly rolls the thunder,
Whereat leap on high the white sea-horses,
Which Boreas himself has begotten
With the light-bounding mares of Erichthon;
And scared the sea-birds silently flutter

Like spectral phantoms from Styx
Whom Charon repulsed from his shadowy boat.

   Poor little merry bark,
Dancing yonder a grim dread dance !
Æolus sends thee his nimblest companions
Who wildly play up for the rollicking frolic ;
One doth whistle, another howls,
While the third plays a rumbling bass—
And the staggering sailor stands at the helm
And steadily scans the compass,
The trembling soul of the vessel ;
And he raises his hands beseeching to heaven :
" Oh, save me, Castor, doughtiest of heroes,
And Pollux, mightiest of boxers ! "

Shipwreck

Hope and Love ! All hopelessly shattered !
And myself, like a corpse,
Grudgingly cast up by the sea,
Am washed on shore,
On the dull naked shore.
Before me surges the wide waste of waters,
Behind me lie but sorrow and anguish,
While over my head sail the clouds,
The shapeless grey daughters of air :

Heine

Who fetch, in buckets of vapour,
Water from ocean,
And drag and drag it in arduous toil,
But to spill it again in the sea,
A dull and tedious employment,
And useless like my own life.
The billows murmur, the sea-gulls scream,
Old memories drift o'er my soul,
Forgotten dreams and faded visions,
Torturingly sweet ones, start forth again.

   A woman lives in the North,
A beautiful woman, queenly beautiful.
Round her cypress-slim limbs
Flows a white and voluptuous garment;
A dark mass of ringlets,
Dark and tender as night,
Falls from her head crowned with tresses,
Encircling dreamily, sweetly
Her sweet pale face;
And forth from her sweet pale face,
Large and mighty, flashes her eye
Like a black burning sun.

   Oh, how often, thou black burning sun,
Transportingly often, have I drunk from thee
Wild flames of inspiration,
Till I staggered and stood all blinded with fire,—
Then a dovelike smile would tremble

Round those haughtily-swelling proud lips,
And those haughtily-swelling proud lips
Breathed words, tender as moonlight,
And sweet as the perfume of roses,—
And my soul spread her wings
And soared and mounted on high, as an eagle!

   Silence, ye birds and ye billows!
All has expired, Love and Hope,
Yea, Hope and Love! I lie on the beach,
A dreary shipwrecked man,
And press my glowing face
On the cold wet sand.

The Setting Sun

THE beauteous sun
Has calmly descended into the ocean;
The restless waters already are dimmed
With gloomy night,
Save where the evening's red
Flushes them golden with flecks of light;
And the swelling murmuring tide
Drives to the shore the white-crested breakers,
That bound and leap,
Like fleecy white flocks,
Which at nightfall the shepherd-boy
Drives home singing.

"How fair is the sun!"
Thus spoke my friend who was walking beside me,
After long pause breaking silence;
And half in joking and half in earnest
He assured me that the sun[1]
Was a lovely woman, who only had married
The ancient sea-god from 'convenance;'
All day long she beams on high,
Joyful and clothed in purple,
Diamond-flashing,
And loved and admired
By all creation,
And delighting the whole creation
With the light and warmth of her glance;
But at night, she is fain, in mute despair,
To return again
To her watery house and the dreary arms
Of her aged husband.
"Indeed, believe me," added my friend,
And smiled and sighed and smiled again—
"They lead down below the tenderest union,
Either they sleep, or they quarrel together;
Then the sea above foams up high,
And the sailors hear in the waves' wild uproar
The old man scolding his wife:
'Thou, the world's round Wanton!
Radiant Coquette!
The livelong day thou glowest for others,

[1] In German, the sun is feminine.

But at night, for me, thou art frosty and tired!
After this curtain lecture
The haughty sun bursts into tears
As a matter of course,
And bewails her lot,
And weeps so bitterly that the sea-god
Suddenly jumps out of bed in despair,
And hastily swims to the ocean's surface
To recover time for breath and reflection.

"Thus saw I him only the other night,
Extending, breast-high, from out the water:
He wore a jersey of yellow flannel,
And a white tasselled nightcap,
And an old wizened face."

The Song of the Oceanides

EVENING shadows fall pale and dim,
And desolate, with his own desolate soul,
A man sits alone on the naked beach,
And gazes with dreary cold look on high,
To the wide and dreary vault of heaven:—
And he looks on the vast and billowy sea,
And his sighs, those sailors of air,
Wander o'er the vast billowy sea,
And thence return desponding;
For the heart wherein they had hoped to anchor

They found fast locked—
And so loudly it groaned, that the white-winged gulls,
In hundreds from their nests in the sand,
Flutter round him affrighted,
And he speaks unto them these laughing words:

" Black-legged Flutterers !
With gleaming wings the ocean skimming,
With crooked bills salt water drinking,
And rancid sealflesh-gorging birds !
Your life is bitter like unto your food !
But I, the happy one, taste but of sweetness,
I taste the dainty rose's sweet perfume,
Of the moonshine-nurtured nightingale-bride ;
I taste yet more sweet and delicious manna,
Sweetmeats filled with whipped cream, forsooth ;
And, sweetest of all, I taste
Sweet love and sweet being beloved.

"She loves me ! She loves me ! the charming maiden ;
Now stands she at home at the balcony window,
And gazes longingly out on the road,
And listens for me—in faith, but she does !
In vain she gazes around and sighs she,
And, sighing, descends she into the garden
And saunters about in fragrance and moonshine,
And speaks to the flowers, and tells them enraptured,
How I, her Beloved, am so engaging,
And so truly charming—in faith, but she does !

Later on in her bed, in her sleep, in her dreams,
My precious image hovers around her,
Yea, even at breakfast time, in the morning.
Shining upon her bread and butter,
She beholds my smiling countenance,
And, lovesick, she eats it—in faith, but she does!"

 Thus he brags and he boasts,
And shrilly the gulls shriek between,
As though giggling in irony cold.
The mists of twilight rise shadowy and dim,
And forth from purple night cloud
Looks forth the lurid uncanny moon.
Louder yet moan and surge the billows,
And forth from the murmuring billowy tide
Sad, like sighing breezes,
Sounds the song of the nymphs of the ocean,
Of the fair and pitiful water maidens;
And above all the others is heard the sweet voice
Of the silver-footed wife of Peleus;
And they sigh and they sing:

 "O fool, thou fool, thou poor bragging fool!
Fool, tortured by grief!
Behold, all thy hopes lie murdered before thee,
The playful children of thy fond heart,
And, alas! thy heart, like Niobe's,
Doth harden to stone;
Black night enshrouds thy head,

And the lightnings of madness flash athwart it,
And thou vauntest for very grief!
O fool, thou fool, thou poor bragging fool,
Stubborn thou art, as was thy forefather,
That mighty Titan, who stole from the Gods
Celestial fire, and gave it to men;
And vulture-tortured, chained to the rocks,
Defied Olympus, defied it, and groaned,
That even we heard it deep down in the sea,
And came to console him with balmy song.
O fool, thou fool, thou poor bragging fool!
And lo! thou art yet more helpless than he,
And prudent it were thou shouldst honour the gods,
And shouldst patiently bear with the load of thy sorrow,
And shouldst bear it with patience, so long, aye, so long,
Till Atlas himself shall lose patience,
And shall hurl from his shoulders the heavy world
Into endless night."

Thus sounded the song of the ocean nymphs,
Of the fair and pitiful water maidens,
Till louder billows o'er-murmured and drowned it—
The moon withdrew behind clouds,
Old Night did yawn,
And I sat long time in the dark and wept.

The Gods of Greece

O DAZZLING full moon! in thy pure light,
Like molten gold doth glitter the sea;
As clear as day, yet in silvery enchantment,
Stretches away the long line of beach;
And up in the pale blue starless sky
White clouds are sailing,
Like colossal statues of gods
Of lustrous marble.

   No! these images never are clouds!
These are themselves, e'en the gods of Hellas,
Who once so joyously reigned o'er the earth,
But now, supplanted and lifeless,
Wander as Phantoms gigantic
Over the midnight sky.

   Strangely dazzled, I wond'ring behold
This airy Pantheon,
And those solemn and silent giant forms,
Drifting in motion dread.
Yon is Kronion, king of the heavens,
Snow-white now are the locks of his head,
Those renowned locks that were wont to shake
Olympus itself;
The extinguished lightning he holds in his hand,
On his countenance lie misfortune and grief,

And still withal his ancient pride.
Those were better times, O Zeus,
When, godlike, thou tookest delight
In youths and nymphs and hecatombs;
But even the gods, they reign not for ever,
And the young supplant the old,
As thou thyself one time didst dethrone
Thy aged father and Titan uncles,
Jupiter Parricida!
Thee, too, proud Juno, I recognize!
Despite all thy jealous anger and fear,
Another has taken the sceptre from thee,
And thou reignest no longer as Queen of Heaven;
And thy big eyes are frozen and dull,
And all powerless droop thy lily arms,
And nevermore shalt thou wreak thy vengeance
On the God-impregnated virgin,
And the miracle-working Son of God.
Thee, too, I recognize, Pallas Athene!
And couldst thou not with thy shield and thy wisdom
Avert the gods' great disaster?
Thee also I know, thee too, Aphrodite,
Once the golden, alas, now of silver!
'Tis true that still the zone's charm doth adorn thee,
Yet secretly dread I thy awful beauty,
And shouldst thou all graciously deign to indulge me
Like other heroes, I'd die of alarm;
A ghoul-like goddess thou seemest to me,
Venus Libitina!

No longer the terrible Ares regards thee
With longing and love.
And sadly gazes Phœbus Apollo,
The youthful, and all silent his lyre,
Which so joyous he swept at the feast of the gods.
Hephæstus gazes still sadder than he,
And, truly, the Halting One never again
Shall fill Hebe's place,
Nor pour out busily in the assembly
The nectar divine. And long has expired
The laughter unquenchable of the gods!

I never have loved you, ye gods!
For odious to me are the Greeks,
And more still the Romans are hateful to me;
But sacred compassion and shuddering pity
Doth thrill my heart,
When I behold you now on high,
Ye deserted gods,
Extinct night-walking Shadows,
Nebulous weak ones, scared by the wind;—
And when I bethink me, how poor and faint-hearted
The new gods are that have conquered you,
The sorry and reigning new gods,
Spitefully glad in sheepskin of meekness,—
Oh, then am I seized with rancour dark,
And I should like to break their new temples,
And fight for you, ye ancient gods,
For you and your good ambrosial right;

Heine

And before your high altars,
Built up again and smoking with worship,
I myself should like to kneel down,
And pray with uplifted hands—

  For, look you, ye ancient gods,
Though in ages gone by, in your combats with men,
You still did side with the conquerors,
Yet man is more generous than you were ever;
And in the combat of gods, I now side
With you, the Conquered.

      *   *   *   *

  Thus I spake, and visibly blushed
On high the pale Cloud Images,
And gazed on me, dying
And sorrow-transformed, and suddenly vanished;
The moon had just hidden
Her face in the clouds rolling nearer;
The ocean foamed,
And triumphantly shone forth from out the dark heavens
The stars eternal.

Questions

By the sea, the dreary nocturnal sea,
Stands a Stripling-Man,
His breast full of sorrow, his head full of doubt,
And with gloomy lips he asks of the waters:

"Oh, solve me the Riddle of Life,
That harrowing, world-old riddle,
Whereon many heads have pondered and brooded;
Heads in caps hieroglyph-scribbled,
Heads in turbans, and heads in black beavers,
Heads periwigged, and a thousand others,
Poor aching human heads—
Tell me—what signifies Man?
Whence has he come? And whither goes he?
Who dwells up on the golden stars?"

The waves they murmur their endless babble,
The wind it blows, and the clouds they wander,
The stars they glitter coldly indifferent,—
And a fool waits for an answer.

The Phœnix

FORTH from the West the Phœnix is flying,
He flies towards the East,
To his Eastern garden retreat,
Where spices grow in perfume and fragrance,
Where palm trees rustle and springs give coolness,
And flying the wondrous bird doth sing:

"She loves him! She loves him!
Within her small heart she carries his likeness,

And secretly, sweetly doth she hide it,
And scarce knows herself!
But in her dreams he standeth before her,
And she weeps and beseeches and kisses his hands,
And calls on his name,
And calling, awakens, and lies sore confused;
Bewildered she rubs her beautiful eyes—
She loves him! She loves him!"

* * * *

Leaning against the mast on the deck,
I stood and heard the song of the bird.
Like dark green horses with silver manes,
Dashed about the white-crested billows;
Like strings of wild swans went flying by,
With gleaming pinions, the Heligoland smacks,
Those Nomads bold of the North Sea!
Overhead, in the deep blue sky
White clouds fluttered their streamers,
And flashed the fair rose of heaven,
The fiery-flowering eternal Sun,
Joyously mirroring him in the sea;—
And heaven and ocean and my own heart
Unceasingly echoed:
"She loves him! She loves him!"

In the Harbour

Happy is he who hath reached the safe harbour,
Leaving behind him the stormy wild ocean,
And now sits cosy and warm
In the good old Town-Cellar of Bremen.

How sweet and homelike the world is reflected,
In the chalice green of a Rhinewine rummer,
And how the dancing microcosm
Sunnily glides down the thirsty throat!
Everything I behold in the glass,
History, old and new, of the nations,
Both Turks and Greeks, and Hegel and Gans,
Forests of citron and big reviews,
Berlin and Shilda, and Tunis and Hamburg;
But, above all, thy image, Beloved,
And thy dear little head on gold-ground of Rhenish!

Oh, how fair, how fair art thou, Dearest!
Thou art fair as the rose!
Not like the Rose of Shiras,
That bride of the nightingale, sung by Hafis;
Not like the Rose of Sharon,
That mystic red rose, exalted by prophets;—
Thou art like the "Rose"[1] of the Bremen Town-Cellar,

[1] A tun of celebrated wine in the "Rathskeller" of Bremen called the "Rose," round which are ranged twelve vats called "the Apostles."

Which is the Rose of Roses;
The older it grows the sweeter it blossoms,
And its breath divine it hath all entranced me,
It hath inspired and kindled my soul;
And had not the Town-Cellar Master gripped me
With firm grip and steady,
I should have stumbled!

   That excellent man! We sat together
And drank like brothers;
We spoke of wonderful mystic things,
We sighed and sank in each other's arms,
And me to the faith of love he converted;—
I drank to the health of my bitterest foes,
And I forgave all bad poets sincerely,
Even as I may one day be forgiven;—
I wept with devotion, and at length
The doors of salvation were opened unto me,
Where the sacred Vats, the twelve Apostles,
Silently preach, yet oh, so plainly,
Unto all nations.

   These be men forsooth!
Of humble exterior, in wooden jerkins,
Yet within they are fairer and more enlightened
Than all the Temple's proud Levites,
Or the courtiers and followers of Herod,
Though decked out in gold and in purple;—
Have I not constantly said so:

Not with the herd of common low people,
But in the best and politest of circles
The King of Heaven was sure to dwell!

Hallelujah! How lovely the whisper
Of Bethel's palm-trees!
How fragrant the myrtles of Hebron!
How sings the Jordan and reels with joy!—
My immortal spirit likewise is reeling,
And I reel in company, and joyously reeling
Leads me upstairs and into the daylight,
That excellent Town-Cellar Master of Bremen.

Thou excellent Town-Cellar Master of Bremen!
Dost see on the housetops the little angels
Sitting aloft, all tipsy and singing?
The burning sun up yonder
Is but a fiery and drunken nose,
The Universe Spirit's red nose;
And round the Universe Spirit's red nose
Reels the whole drunken world.

Epilogue

As grow on a wheat field the ears and haulms.
Thus grow and expand in the spirit of man
His thoughts.
But the tender thoughts of sweet love

Are as the red and blue flowers
Gaily blooming between.

   Ye cornflowers and poppies !
The churlish reaper as useless reviles you,
Wooden flails mockingly thresh you,
Even the poor wayfarer,
Whom the sight of you cheers and rejoices,
Doth shake his head,
And call you fair weeds.
But the village maiden,
Weaving her garlands,
Loves you and plucks you
And adorns with you her tresses,
And thus adorned she hies to the dance,
Where pipe and tabor sweetly are sounding ;
Or to the trysting hawthorn,
Where the voice of her sweetheart is music yet sweeter
Than pipe e'en or tabor.

Nicolaus Lenau

Sedge Songs

I.

FAINTLY sets the sun o'er yonder,
    Tired falls the day asleep,
And the willows trail their streamers
    In these waters still and deep.

Flow, my bitter tears, flow ever,
    All I love I leave behind ;
Sadly whisper here the willows,
    And the reed shakes in the wind.

Into my deep lonely sufferings
    Tenderly you shine afar,
As athwart these reeds and rushes
    Trembles soft yon evening star.

II.

Oft at eve I love to saunter
   Where the sedge sighs drearily,
By entangled hidden footpaths,
   Love! and then I think of thee.

When the woods gloom dark and darker,
   Sedges in the nightwind moan,
Then a faint mysterious wailing
   Bids me weep, still weep alone.

And methinks I hear it wafted,
   Thy sweet voice, remote yet clear,
Till thy song, descending slowly,
   Sinks into the silent mere.

III.

Angry sunset sky,
   Thunder-clouds o'erhead,
Every breeze doth fly,
   Sultry air and dead.

From the lurid storm
   Pallid lightnings break,
Their swift transient form
   Flashes through the lake.

And I seem to see
    Thyself, wondrous nigh,—
Streaming wild and free
    Thy long tresses fly.

Mist

Grey envious mist, thou still dost hide
    Valley and river's run,
The forest on the mountain side,
    And every gleam of sun.

Take thou into thy sombre night
    This earth so broad and vast;
Take all that makes my soul so sad,
    Take, too, away the Past!

Julius Mosen

The Crossbill

I.

FULL often with the fowler
  In tranquil peace was I
All night long in the forest,
  Nor ever closed an eye.

Of every bird the fowler
  Some wondrous legend told,
Inside that dusky chamber
  Grew dazzling fairy gold.

But in yon wicker basket,
  That bird with purple wing
And crooked beak doth comfort
  In all affliction bring.

I've now a bitter yearning,
  A silent aching pain,

Yon bird I heard so often,
   To hear once more again.

Methinks, could I but hear it
   Sing, in my soul's distress,
Perchance 'twould still the beating
   Of my heart's restlessness.

II.

When the flowers long have faded,
   Ere the dreary winter's rest,
Lo! a bird upon the fir-tree
   Only now has built its nest.

In this wintry desolation,
   Sits the bird as red as blood,
Under frozen icy branches
   Hatching tenderly its brood.

Strange a bird art thou, O Crossbill!
   And I often think of thee,
When the world so cold and empty
   As a wilderness I see.

III.

High upon the cross our Saviour
   Hung, His eyes towards Heaven bent,
When He feels a gentle pricking
   On His hand, all torn and rent.

Mağen

Christ, by everyone forsaken,
   Here this little bird doth see
Striving earnestly to loosen
   One harsh nail in charity.

And with blood bedewed and sprinkled,
   Never resting, it doth seek
From the Cross to free the Saviour
   With its tiny tender beak.

Then the Lord He spake in mercy:
   " Be for evermore thou blest;
Henceforth ever shall adorn thee
   Sign of cross and bloodstained crest."

And the bird was called the Crossbill—
   Covered o'er with blood so bright,
It doth sing all sad and strangely
   In the forest's leafy night.

IV.

Like this bird, I, too, am striving,
   But, alas! without avail,
From my poor and tortured country
   To wrench out a cruel nail.

But all drenchèd with its bitter
   Tears, and stainèd with its blood,
In despair I now am singing
   Mournfully within the wood.

Wail aloud, ye gloomy pine-trees,
   Torrents, rush with angry roar,
That my song may not re-echo
   From these mountains to the shore.

Eduard Mœrike

"One little hour ere day"

THE while I sleeping lay
One little hour ere day,
Before my window on the tree
A swallow sang this song to me,
One little hour ere day.

" Now listen to my lay,
Thy lover I betray!
The while I sing this song to thee,
Another maiden kisseth he
One little hour ere day."

Oh me, no further say!
Ah hush, no more betray!
Fly, swallow, from my sill away.
Ah, love and faith, a dream are they
One little hour ere day!

Suum Cuique

ANINKA dances
In rapid measure
Upon the greensward,
    How fair was she!

With drooping lashes,
With eyes so modest,
The modest maiden—
    She drives me wild!

Lo, springs a button
From off her jacket,
A golden button,
    I caught it up!

And deemed it wondrous,
A sweet strange omen,
But all sarcastic
    Jegór doth smile,

As who should tell me:
Mine is the jacket
And all it covers,
Mine is the maiden;
    The button—thine!

Ferdinand Freiligrath

Sea Fable

HIGH and dry upon the seashore
    Lies the helpless fishing-smack;
From the mast the net is hanging,
    Dripping still, all wet and black.

Yon barefooted boy is trying
    All its meshes o'er with care;
Fishes in the sun are drying
    On the wooden framework there.

Parched, the arid plain is gazing
    On the sea, a Tantalus;
Like a mighty silver crescent
    Flashes great Oceanus.

Every billow, gray and salty,
    As upon the beach it broke,
As if greeting with its crested
    Head, it nodded, and then spoke:

"On the beach I love to murmur,
   Love to lick the firm hard sand,
Coloured shells and starfish gladly
   Do I fling upon the land.

"Much I love to see the wild gorse
   Straggling grow about the plain;
Here do I forget how gloomy
   Is without, the boundless main,

"Which the stormy tempest lashes,
   Where the Norsemen fishing go,
Where the Arctic and the German
   Oceans both together flow.

"Neither buoy nor blazing beacon
   Watch on yonder waters keep,
And the Kraken rises nightly
   From his caverns in the deep.

"Stiff with scales, a rigid island,
   See him steer along the shore;
Terrified, the skiffs seek safety,
   And the fisher grasps his oar.

"A huge plain doth he resemble;—
   Combat-ready lies he now,
And his back with warts is covered
   As with hillocks—high and low.

Freiligrath

"Calmly floats he—on a sudden,
   With a hissing fierce and dread
Darts on him the great Sea-serpent;
   Moss is growing on its head.

"When the two are struggling, when their
   Gory crests do wave, I ween
Ne'er more wondrous and more fearful
   Sight on ocean yet was seen.

"Lonely, horrible, and gloomy
   Is the distant dreary main;—
Much I love to see the wild gorse
   Straggling grow about the plain."

Roland

A REVERIE

'Twas in the wood; through silent glades we go,
Where hides herself the faint and stricken doe,
Where, quivering, through the leaves shoot gleams of day,
Where horn and axe in answering echoes play.

Deep silence reigns; only the turtle-dove
Coos overhead her murmuring plaints of love,
The spring but bubbles, and the ancient trees
Scarce rustle, wrapt in dreamy reveries.

The beech makes moan, the ash is gently stirred,
Far off the clanging of a forge is heard,
My staff's harsh grate as 'gainst a stone it rung,—
This is the mountain-forests' native tongue !

I heard its voice with throb akin to weeping,
Into my greenwood joy sweet pain came creeping,
Rock, forest, solitude, these all unite
To touch my inmost soul with magic might.

I thought of yonder pass where Roland fell ;
Would God that such a fate were mine as well !
A life of wrestling, flight of Saracen,
And the death-signal in the rocky glen !

The battle roars ; I boldly take my stand,
Long time my sword has glittered in my hand ;
Early and late by foes I'm sore beset,
My horn, my Poesy, is slumbering yet.

It rests and slumbers gravely on my right,
It rests and dreams, whilst I myself do fight ;
Only at times, a wild and broken note,
To cheer the fray, bursts fitful from its throat.

What are my songs, in sooth, but signals all
To aid my courage and to cheer my soul ?
Wild savage chords, rude sounds, which, when at rest,
Harshly escape from out my labouring breast.

Freiligrath

What other theme should warriors' souls delight?
Grasp firm your sword an you would win the fight!
Your rage and anger breathe into your arms,
And let your bugle rest from war's alarms.

Triumphant lays the conqueror can afford;—
Wake you the iron clash of sword on sword!
Signals?—So be't!—A challenge short and shrill
Then boldly utter over dale and hill.

But only then a full triumphant blast,
When the proud Saracen lies slain at last,
When you have hurled your mighty enemy,
All armed in mail, upon the ground to die.

Within a pass like this and Ronceval
Dead at your feet the giant then shall fall;
But you yourself are wounded to the death,
Then sound your bugle with your dying breath!

And while your life-blood ebbing fast you feel,
To Charlemagne send forth a last appeal,
One piercing cry—the revelation true
Of all you wished and strove and dared to do!

Which in quick breathless gasps shall all reveal,
What, in the strife, your pride forbade to tell,
One last confession, one last menace bold,—
The signature to your whole life behold!

Hark, what a sound! The mountains ring again,
Upon your neck starts purple every vein.
Afar, each comrade hears your cry of need,
Tremblingly hears it, quickly turns his steed.

The Emperor comes, the Paladins, in haste,
Alas! your blood wells forth in fearful waste:
Encircling you in silence they stand round,
Your eye is glazed—your bugle gives no sound.

Then stifled murmurs through the valley spread:
"*Life's Battle!* yea, it is a giant dread!
Honour to him who nobly waged the fight,
Bury him thus, his bugle in his right!"—

Ha! Such a fate!—Sighing, the ash is stirred,
Far off the clanging of a forge is heard,
Black thunder-clouds rush by in angry mass,
And dark and darker glooms the mountain-pass.

The Flowers' Revenge

WRAPT in deep repose, the maiden
  On the bed's soft couch is lying,
Gently droops her silken eyelash,
  Crimson her hot cheek is dyeing.

Freiligrath

Glittering on the chair of rushes
    Stands a vase of rich adorning,
Flowers are gathered in its chalice
    Fresh and fragrant but this morning.

Stifling, sultry heat has settled,
    Brooding, o'er the silent room,
Closed are lattices and windows,
    Twilight darkens into gloom.

Quiet now, and deepest silence !
    Sudden, hark ! a soft low rustling !
Leaves and flowers gently whisper,
    Lisping low with eager bustling.

From the flowers, lo ! are rising
    Fairy forms so light and slender ;
Thinnest mist their floating garments,
    Shields and crowns they bear in splendour.

From the Rose's blushing bosom
    Steps a woman, tall and fair ;
Pearls are glistening like dewdrops
    In her loose and fluttering hair.

From the Monkhood's iron helmet,
    From its foliage darkly gleaming,
Strides a knight of dauntless courage,
    Sword and armour brightly beaming.

O'er his helmet waves the plumage
   Of the heron, silver-pale;
From the Lily floats a maiden,
   Thinnest gossamer her veil.

From the spotted Tiger Lily
   Issues forth an Arab bold,
On his turban green is blazing
   Fierce the crescent's arch of gold.

Boldly from the Crown Imperial
   Steps a sceptre-bearer royal;
From the azure Iris follow
   Sword-girt all his hunters loyal.

From the leaves of the Narcissus
   Gloomy-eyed a youth doth slip,
Pressing hot and burning kisses
   On the maiden's cheek and lip.

But around her couch, the others
   Wildly dance and wheel again,
Round in mazy circles flying,
   Singing angrily this strain:

"From the earth, hast thou, O maiden,
   Torn us with a cruel hand,
That we now must fade and languish
   In this painted flower-stand.

Freiligrath

"Oh, how happy were we, resting
   On the breast of Mother Earth,
Where, through tender foliage glancing,
   Sunbeams kissed us oft in mirth;

"Where soft summer breezes fanned us,
   Bending low our stems so airy,
Where at night our leafy dwellings
   We did quit, as elf or fairy.

"Heavenly rain and dew refreshed us,
   Here we droop in stagnant water—
Lo, we fade, but ere we perish
   Maiden! we'll avenge our slaughter!"

Finished is their song, as bending
   O'er the sleeper they bow lowly.
With the old and sultry silence
   Comes again that whispering slowly.

What a rushing, what a murmuring,
   How the maiden's cheek doth glow,
How the spirits breathe upon her,
   How the perfumes faintly flow!

Now the sun salutes her chamber,
   Scaring every phantom shade;
On the couch is calmly sleeping,
   Cold and dead, the loveliest maid.

Tinged her cheek with faintest crimson,
    She, herself a faded flower,
Rests beside her faded sisters,
    Murdered by their fragrant power.

On the Sea

"Alone on the tranquil sea I ride,
On its surface is scarcely a ripple or frown,
On the sands far beneath me, in stately pride
Shines the old o'erwhelmèd town.

"In hoary times did a king expel,
As the legends say, his child fair and good,
Then far o'er the mountains she went to dwell
With seven dwarfs in a wood.

"And when, through her wicked stepmother, she
Had died from some baneful poison's might,
She was laid by the tiny community
In a crystal coffin of light.

"And thus she lay in her snow-white dress,
Adorned with flowers fragrant and fair,
Thus lay she in all her loveliness,
And could ever be seen by them there.

Freiligrath

"So, too, O Julin, in thy coffin of glass
As a corpse dost thou lie, decked in glorious array,
The flowing waves, as transparent they pass,
Thy palaces' lustre display.

"Up tower thy spires gloomy and tall,
And their mourning in sadness and silence declare,
The archèd gateway breaks through the wall,
The church windows gorgeously flare.

"But in all this magnificence solemn and still
Not a human footstep, no mirth, no song,
Through the streets, o'er the market the fish at their will
Slowly drift by in uncouth throng.

"Full into the windows and into the doors
They stupidly stare with dull glazed eye,
And there the inhabitants sleepy and dumb
In their houses of stone they descry.

"But I will descend, and I will restore
With th' inspiring power of my living breath
The sunken splendour and might of yore,
And break the enchantment of death.

"Once more let life with its bustle and trade
Fill the market space and the pillared hall;
Now open your eyes, Oh each fair maid!
And bless the long dream ye all.

"Down, downwards!"—he stops, nor further rows,
His hands and arms sink rigidly down.
O'er his head the waters silently close,
And at length he salutes the town.

He lives where the pearl and the amber glow,
He lives in the houses forgotten long;—
The splendour and glory of Eld below,
On the surface a fisher-song!

The Death of the Leader

"From the sails the fog is dripping,
    O'er the bay the mist doth fly;
Light the lantern at the mast-head,
    Dull the water—dull the sky;
Funeral weather!—Heads uncover!—
    Wives and children, young and old,
Come and pray, for in the cabin
    You a dead man shall behold."

And the German peasants follow
    Their New England captain's tread,
In the lowly cabin entering
    With a sad and drooping head.
They, who for a home, a new one,
    Crossed the ocean vast and gray,
In his shroud they see the old man
    Who has led them till to-day.

Freiligrath

Who, from boards of fir and pinewood,
    Built a hut that floated free
To the Rhine adown the Neckar,
    From the Rhine down to the sea.
Who, white-haired and heavy-hearted,
    Sadly left his father's land,
Saying: "Let us rise and wander,
    Let us make a covenant;—

"Let us all break up towards evening,
    Westward doth our dawn flush bright;
Over yonder let us settle,
    There where freedom holds her right;
There we'll sow our sweat in furrows
    Where 'tis not an idle seed,
There we'll till the soil, where each one
    That has ploughed shall earn his meed.

"Let us carry each his homestead
    Far into the forests dark,
Let me be in the Savannahs,
    Let me be your Patriarch!
Let us live as lived the shepherds
    In the Bible's olden lay,
And our journey's fiery pillar
    Be the light that burns for aye.

"On this light I place reliance,
    It will never guide us wrong,

In my grandsons I see proudly
    Future generations strong;
Ah!—I once had hoped my country
    Would receive my weary dust,
For my children's sake I grasp yet
    Scrip and staff with hopeful trust.

Up then! And from Goshen follow
    Yon bright pioneering star!"
Ah, he viewed, a second Moses,
    Canaan only from afar!
He has died upon the ocean,
    Both he and his wishes cease,
Disappointment or Fulfilment
    Cannot now disturb his peace.

Orphaned now the band, about to
    Sink their leader in the deep;
Awed the little children hide them,
    Silently their mothers weep;
And the men, with anxious bosom,
    Gaze upon the distant shore,
Where this pious one—ah, never!
    At their side shall wander more.

"From the sails the mist is dripping,
    Fog hangs heavy on the wave,
Pray ye! Let the ropes be slackened,
    Give him to his billow grave."

Freiligrath

Tears are shed and waves are foaming,
    Seagulls flit with angry cry;
He who tilled the earth his life long,
    In the sea doth calmly lie.

The Water Gueux

A CORPSE the German Ocean
Has cast upon the land;
A fisherman has seen it,
And hastens to the strand.

From out the scarf he presses
The blood and brine so red,
He opes the dead man's armour,
Lifts the beaver off his head;

His beaver gay with crescent,
With feathers soiled and creased;
Sand cleaves around the inscription:
" Much rather Turk than Priest!"

Why bearest thou on shore him,
To loose his armour's clasp?
No longer sword and rudder
This warrior's hand shall grasp;

For when the Spaniard's bulwarks
He clutched with sinewy fist,
In grappling, with a hatchet
They smote it from the wrist.

Down fell he plunging backwards ;—
The sea with sullen roar
Received him, and yet bleeding
Has cast him here ashore.

The brave and knightly body
Floated to Zealand's strand ;
On Friesland's coast a maiden
Doth find the mangled hand.

An anchor black and dripping
With ocean's humid air,
A rough and rusty tide-mark,
Is standing upright there.

As, leaning on the anchor,
A gleaming sail to see,
Or gaily fluttering pennon,
—Image of hope is she !—

Lo, what comes on the breakers?
A hand as if to greet !
The cold and stiffened fingers
Have touched her very feet.

Freiligrath

Upon one finger glistens
A stone as red as blood,
And on it are engraven
A falcon and lion good.

No longer shall the falcon
His pinions spread on high ;
This hand it is the lion's,
Who at her feet did lie ;

Whose brow she will no longer
Entwine with garlands green ;—
Already twilight darkens ;
Her face cannot be seen.

I cannot see if dimly
She sheds a burning tear,
But I can see her trembling
Lift up the hand in fear,

Within her white veil hiding
The relic stained with gore,
And homewards faintly gliding,
—Image of hope no more !—

# A Century of German Lyrics

Henry

A DREAR and empty room; the evening sun's last ray
Through the dim windows pale and sickly breaks its way,
Through faded panes it faintly glances.
A camp-bed and a chair, a table too—and see
A coffin yonder—nay! quake not, but follow me!
Let us behold two countenances.

A maiden's image here admiringly behold!
What eyes! What sweetness! Ah, what locks of waving
    gold!
Lips whereon love doth seem to tremble!
An azure girdle clasps her slim waist daintily;
Should ever I be loved, I pray to God that she
This maiden's portrait may resemble!

Now turn to yonder bier; from shroud so white and dim
A youth's face lies upturned; his features stiff and grim
Scowl forth, with pain and sorrow wasted;
With deep and deadly grief his silent lips are drawn,
But that the tempest fierce within should ne'er be known,
To seal these lips in death he hasted!

Turn back the winding-sheet:—dost see the dagger shine
Bloodstained within his hand? Let not faint heart be thine!

Freiligrath

—His heart doth sheathe this poniard chilly!—
Once more cast on this face so joyous-fair thine eye,
Then on this agonized!—Now come!—But ask not why
This last sad face doth rest so stilly!

The Fir-Tree

On the mountain's highest summit
    Straight and green the Fir doth grow,
Stretching forth its roots and fibres
    Through the creviced rocks below.

Towards the highest cloud-banks soaring,
    Lo, its topmost branches sweep,
As if them, of birdlike swiftness,
    They would grasp and firmly keep.

For the clouds, a hundred-shapen,
    Streaming, tattered, rent in twain,
Are the Fir-tree's needle cushions,
    Vast grey masses, big with rain.

Far within its gnarled fibres,
    Dank and brown with clinging earth,
Live the dwarfs of tiny stature,
    Madcaps they in pranks and mirth.

Without ladders, without buckets,
   They the mountain's depth explore;
In those wondrous mines, the metals
   Melt they into precious ore.

Tangled, do its roots hang downward
   To the caverns deep below,
There beholding diamonds glitter,
   And the gold's rich yellow glow.

But on high, its shady branches
   Love to see a scene more fair,
See the sun through foliage glancing,
   Watch the Spirit's stir and care,

Who, with clever dwarfs, his helpmates,
   In this lonely mountain range
Everything doth keep in order,
   All doth govern and arrange;

Often too, at change of solstice,
   After nightfall rushes by,
Round his loins a shaggy deerskin,
   In his fist a pine-tree high.

Catching every note that's uttered
   By each songster's tender beak,
Not a word the Fir-tree loseth
   What the bubbling brook doth speak;

Freiligrath

Doth behold the forest creatures'
    Household, in calm happiness,—
Oh, what peace, what ample riches
    In this shady wilderness!

Man is distant.—Nought but red-deer's
    Tracks upon the mossy ground;—
Ah! well may'st thou, all exulting,
    Scatter far thy cones around.

Ah! well may'st thou sprinkle fragrant
    Drops of amber resin bright,
And adorn thy stiff and dark green
    Hair, with dew in the morning's light!

Ah! well may'st thou whisper softly,
    Aye, or roar defiance free;
On the lonely mountain waving,
Green and strong the storm-wind braving,
    Fir-tree! could I change with thee!

From out the frigate tapering
    The tall mast lightly rears,
With sail and shroud and pennon;
    'Tis bent with weight of years.

The foaming wave it addresses
    With loud and angry wail;
"What use to me this garment
    Of white and flowing sail?

"What use to me this rigging,
   These flags that sport in the wind?
A secret yearning draws me
   To the forest left behind!

"In early youth they felled me,
   And brought me to the strand,
To navigate the ocean
   And see each foreign land.

"I've sailed the main, beholding
   Sea-kings upon their throne,
Both fair and swarthy nations
   I saw in every zone.

"Rock-nourished moss in Iceland
   Far northwards I did greet,
With palms in southern islands
   I have held converse sweet.

"But evermore I'm longing
   For yon mountain grown with pine,
Where in the dwarfs' dominions
   My hairy roots did twine!

"Oh glades, so brightly flowered,
   Oh greenwood, glad and free;
Oh life, so sweet and dreamy,
   How far, how far are ye!"

Freiligrath

Africa

YE zones, so strange and wondrous,
Thou distant magic land,
Where swarthy men are roving,
Burned by the sun's fierce brand;
Where all things glow and sparkle,
Where the sun's golden beam
The genuine gold doth darken
That flashes bright in every stream.

Thy forests dark and deserts
Are present to my view,
Thy feathery palms are mirrored
In lakes of deepest blue;
The wild beasts' roar is sounding
From cleft and cavern black,
With heavy bales and costly,
The Arab loads his camel's back.

There, too, the curly negro
Gold dust in rivers seeks,
And there Mount Atlas gravely
Rears heaven-supporting peaks;
The sunlight tinges brightly
Its crags with radiant blush,
While elephants gray and sombre
With ponderous step the meadows crush.

To dip his mane in the river
The lion stoopeth down,
And swiftly as the lightning
Canoes dart, light and brown ;
They pass o'er depths securely,
And dates and rosin bear,
And from the waves dark faces,
All dripping and all wet appear.

Oh zone, so hot and glowing,
Queen of the earth art thou !
Sand is thy garment flowing,
The sun doth crown thy brow ;
Of gold, thou queenly woman,
Are all the clasps and rings,
That fasten with fiery splendour
The garment to thy burning limbs.

The strand, with rocks and quicksands,
Naked and parched with heat,
Cut into shapes phantastic
Is a footstool for thy feet ;
The ocean far beneath it,
Its edge doth hem and braid,
Washing thy sandals, foaming,
As an anxious and a willing maid.

On dazzling mats of scarlet
Thou liest thoughtful and calm,

Freiligrath

The spotted panthers are licking
The fingers of thy left palm;
While skilfully thy right hand,
Sparkling with jewels rare,
Into a tress is twisting
The lion's mane of yellow hair;

And then again untwining it,
Into a five-toothed prong,
Dost comb the hair's dense masses,
His tawny back along;
His flanks are proudly heaving,—
Anon, with the same hand
Commandingly thou scarest
The slim giraffes across the sand.

Upon thy shoulder sitting,
In his plumage bright display,
Chattering and shrilly screaming,
Perches a parrot gay;
He lays his beak so crooked
Against thy listening ear,
With strident voice and ringing
Relates he stories strange to hear.

A silken turban, broidered
With flowers, decks thy hair:
A rich and costly necklace,
Such as Sultanas wear,

Of thousand links close knitted
To chain compact and sound,
With golden coil encircles
Thy neck which sun and heat have browned.

Who is there, that has seen thee
In all thy splendour quite?
Dense forests ever screen thee,
Waving with leafy night
Before thy golden crescent,
Before thy cheek's rich bloom,
Before thy lips of scarlet,
Before thine eye which flashes gloom.

None, none have yet beheld thee,
Oh Queen, from face to face,
Although brave suitors many
Advanced with fearless pace,
To lift the veil that covers
Thy brow with mystic fold,—
Ah, with their life atoned they,
The attempt they ventured all too bold.

From off thy throne arising,
With menace dread to see:
" Arouse ye, oh my lions,
Tear him, and fight for me;
Oh sun, thy living fire
From cloudless tent on high,

Freiligrath

Hurl down on the offender
With scorching ardour, hot and dry!

"Subdue his strength, ye vapours,
With sultry poisonous breath,
And let at every palm-tree
A javelin threaten death;
Ye curly-headed negroes,
Haste, bring to me his blood,
Let fly your poisonous arrows,
And take an aim full sure and good!"

Then up doth bound the lion,
Roaring with fierce delight,
And strikes his paw unwieldy
In the breast of the hapless white;
From every bush a warrior
With hideous grin doth leap,
And with its breath of poison
Simoom the desert plain doth sweep.

His spur the Jolof presses
Deep in his charger's side;
How can the fainting pale-face
Such rage as this abide?
All gashed and gory, sinking
A corpse upon the sand,
He cruelly hath perished,
Oh dread Sultana, through thy hand!

Thee, whom he fain desired
To disclose to every eye,
And who didst therefore bear him
Displeasure kindled high;
Thee, in thy sanctuary,
He would have glorified,
Wherefore didst thou deter him
To publish thine own fame and pride?

The negro kings who saw thee
Thirst for the white man's blood,
Now offer it unto thee
In humble suppliant mood;
The golden bowl doth brandish,
Flashing in blood-red sheen,
That many a drop of crimson
Is sprinkled on thy veil of green.

Thy swelling lips thou pressest
Upon the vessel's rim,
On the yellow sand thou gazest
With savage smile and grim;
The corpse before thee is lying,
Fiercely the sun doth sting;
Through ages and through nations
Thy murdered suitors' fame shall ring!

Freiligrath

Leviathan

"Thou didst divide the sea by thy strength; thou brakest the heads of the dragons in the waters. Thou brakest the heads of Leviathan in pieces, and gavest him to be meat to the people inhabiting the wilderness."—Psalm lxxiv.

'TWAS in the early autumn-time, I wandered forth upon the strand,
My temples bare, my eyes downcast, the songs of David in my hand:
The sea was rough, the tide rolled in, a fresh east wind was whistling high,
On the horizon, white of sail, westwards a ship was flying by.

And as I, in King David's book, now skimming and now gazing round,
Had come unto the passage that prophetic o'er this poem is found,
I saw three fishing smacks approach, which drifting slowly onwards bore,
Their dusky sails furled close, towards the lonely and deserted shore.

Behind them, dipping in the waves, an inky mass does float along,
A giant monster of the sea; 'twas fastened to a cable strong;

Loud creak the spars, the sullen surge beats on the shore, the anchor's cast,
The fishing vessels with their prize upon the beach are hauled at last.

And now in numbers, to the call of husbands and of brothers, haste
The people of the wilderness from out their dwellings in the waste;
They gaze on ocean's mighty son, his body slit with fearful gash,
They gaze upon his shattered head, whose rays no more to heaven shall flash.

But few years since the ice-bound Pole gave birth to this its dripping son;
A novice yet, he lost his way on to this shallow coast and dun;
Sandbanks forbade him his return back to the open sea to take,
And with a fisher's spear the Lord this young sea-giant's head doth break.

And round the bleeding animal they shouted, and it seemed to me
As though with fierce contemptuous eye he looked on their unfeeling glee;
Methought his crimson bubbling blood was ebbing forth in angry flood;
Methought he muttered to the storm, "Oh, despicable human brood!

Freiligrath

"Oh, puny dwarfs, who but o'erreached the giant with deceit
    at last,
Pitiful clods, who fain must shun my watery empire deep and
    vast ;
Weak mortals, who but venture forth in hollow bark upon
    the sea,
Like to the wretched oyster, that ne'er from its shell apart
    can be !

"Oh, drear inhospitable coast ! oh, drear and empty living
    there !
Oh, dreary people ! How they shook when first my snorting
    they did hear !
How comfortless their hovels mean upon the naked beach do
    lie !
But art thou better much than they, oh Poet, who dost see
    me die ?

"I would I were where ocean ends, and where the world
    doth cease to be,
Where, crashing through the darkness float icebergs in frozen
    majesty ;
I would a swordfish, whetting there his knife on ice so white
    and clear,
Would flash it swiftly through my breast—at least, I should
    not perish here !"

'Twas in the early autumn-time, a fresh east wind was whist-
    ling high,
On the horizon, white of sail, westwards a ship was flying by ;

I turned aside, I threw me down upon the sand :—the Lord
    doth give
The giant's broken head as meat to them that in the desert
    live.

The Dreadnought Hospital

Across the Thames' flagged surface behold
Through the forest of vessels yon vessel old ;
Its planks are tainted with death and sigh,
Its pennon is black which floats on high.

How different but short time ago,
O'er the seas it shed the matchlock's glow ;
'Tis a ship of the line used to sea-fight's roar,
Once fourscore guns and Nelson it bore.

'Tis the floating hospital of the fleet :
In the gun-room bed beside bed you greet,
From the ceiling the pendant lamp sheds glow
On the death-pale ranks of the sick below.

A gloomy band ! Every breath a groan !
They rave of the sea and their native zone !
Their fevered frenzy wings forth its way
To foreign climes with phantastic sway.

Freiligrath

Bold rovers they from every land !
From the shores of Sind, from the Neva's strand,
From the heights where mule and llama toil,
The wind has drifted them many a mile.

Their foreheads glow ! The sea ! The world !
Shattered obelisk—Blockhouse—Tents unfurled !
The caravan's thunder ! The ocean blue !
Wherever you fly, I will follow too.

On then ! The Negro starts from his bed,
His sinewy arms he tosses o'erhead ;
His last wild fever-dream breaks way :
" To horse, to the lion hunt, away ! "

The Finn's dull eye on the lamp doth brood :
" From the clouds I see it dripping blood !
The Torneo Valley's pine-trees dun
Are bathed in the glow of the midnight sun ! "

On linen pillow, behold, close by
A countenance bronzed by a southern sky ;
With parching lip and hot dry hand,
'Tis a Spaniard from the Duero strand.

With his rolling eye that shall break anon,
His phantom dream wildly he gazes on :—
Towards the deep blue vault of a Spanish sky
The Alhambra rears its turrets high ;

The rose blooms red, the fountain purls,
Castagnettes and the song of Spanish girls,
Their locks flash like jets of raven flame,
The fandango trembles athwart his frame!

Now hark, a song! Crimea's son!
He bids his horse swim through the Don;
He urges it through the sultry track
Which the traveller crosses on camel's back;

His horse he through the Don doth steer,—
In the Steppes a spring is gushing clear;
Where doth fill her pitcher the Russian maid
His charger's fiery course he stayed.

He must go where Odessa's wimples fly,
A song, a kiss, a last good-bye!
Where his steed he watereth in the plain,
He sings a wild and tender strain.

'Tis a Russian song, 'tis a minor strain,
Full of love and full of a yearning pain;
Like a sword it pierces sharp and clear,
The dying man sings it dread to hear.

It trembles across from bed to bed,—
The Chinese doth rouse from his torpor dead;
With his narrow eyes he glances around,
"How hollow the Porcelain Tower doth sound!"

Freiligrath

The Hindoo starts with listening ear:
"How the Ganges murmurs and rushes near!
How proudly the palm trees wave on high!
How the dress of the Bayadère doth fly!"

The Brazilian sailor lifts his hand:
"Hark the breakers booming against the land!
'Tis the ocean lashes, wild, hissing, and free,
The ponderous flags of Janeiro's quay!"

Sea foam, the Steppes, the Bayadère!
O'er each pillow a different dream is there!
From each burning brain there issues bright
Another image forth into the night!

Ye flaming fires, from south and north,
From twenty brains fierce blazing forth,
Be exorcised! Stand in your dazzling glare,
An Orbis Pictus, unique and rare.

'Gainst headlands, Ocean, thy waves let dash,
Gleam forth, ye snowfields, with icy flash;
Shed your leaves, bananas, o'er Ganges' wave,
Oh, Desert, your dust in the Niger lave!

To the powder-room! Let each foreign race,
With seething brain, in the fight take place!
Into the fogs of old England throw
The grenade of fever frenzy aglow!

With its shell, wild bursting, lurid and grand,
Let them storm it as their native land;
Through the frigate let it hiss and fly,
Till on death-beds it pauses, to sink and die!

Till it flashes and bursts! Behold, 'tis done!
It expires with many a pang and groan!
In their shrouds lie the fallen—the death-dew damp
On their brows—their fist closed in iron cramp!

Their throbbing temples as cold as snow!
Their skulls dead embers!—Even so!
The smile that around your lips doth play,
Confesses you victors in the fray.

It shows that you gained the land once more,
Which you left when you gaily pushed from shore;
That, blissfully dreaming, anchor you cast,
Where, parting, you uttered your farewell last;

Where you waved your hat in fond farewell;—
The frigate rocks and the tide doth swell,
The coffins are lowered, the boats push ashore,
A volley salutes them with sullen roar.

All you, who afar did hither roam,
Have found by the Thames a last still home;
The daisies star your turf of green—
A tomb of nations this, I ween.

If every nation that gave them birth
Were now to appear on this strip of earth,
Were to utter its death-wail loud and long,
What country would hear such another song !

From bursting throats hear it rise and swell,
Wild Indian shriek and Malayan yell !
In spirit I hear it rend Night's shroud,
A roar of the Universe, piercing and loud !

Do you hear it too, ye sleepers below?
No answer !—Whispering the night winds blow ;
From afar comes the roar of London's town—
Dark flies the flag o'er the river brown.

On the Drachenfels

High stood I on the Drachenfels,
I bit my lip, my eye flashed proudly,
From cliff and crag with joyous yells
My pointer roused glad echoes loudly ;
He flew before, he leaped and ran,
As though some game he were pursuing,
But I looked forth, a joyful man,
The scene beneath me lost in viewing.

In luscious glory of its vine
Of purple and of yellow cluster,
I saw the Valley of the Rhine,
Arch, like a goblet green of lustre ;
A chalice rare !—Tradition dreams
Upon its brink on ruins hoary ;
The wine that in the goblet foams—
Love and Romance, renowned in story !

Lo, how it sparkles ! joust and fight !
Cheeks glow and flush, and hearts beat madly,
Helmet and casque are flashing bright.
And fresh fair wounds are trickling gladly ;
While on yon turret pensive stands
To whom are lowered lance and crest ;—
Wherefore am I thus strangely moved ?
What sweet foreboding thrills my breast ?

Wild Flowers

ALONE I strolled, where the Rhine stream rolled,
On each hedge was the wild rose glowing,
And through the air, the perfume rare
Of the blooming vine was blowing.
The poppies red their brilliance spread,
The corn to the south wind was bending,
Over Roland's hill a falcon shrill
With his cry the air was rending.

Freiligrath

In mine ear there rung the old sweet song:
"Oh, were I a wild young falcon!"
Oh, thou melody, as a falcon shy,
And as bold, too, as a falcon!
Who will sing and try? To the sun on high
Shall the song on its wings upwave me,
'Gainst a window small, against bars withal,
With my pinions I'll flutter bravely.

Where you see a rose, where a curtain blows,
Where skiffs on the shore are lying,
Where two eyes of brown the stream gaze down,
I fain would be flying, flying!
There with talon strong, and my wildwood song,
At her feet I would fain be sitting,
Encircling now full proudly her brow
With soft and tender greeting!

Oh, but well I sang, and full well I ran,
But no wings could I unfold then;
And my heart was sore, as the ears I tore
Off the stems of the grain so golden;
Bending bough and bush, rending reed and rush,
I ceased not from tearing and grasping,
Till breathless and worn, and my hands all torn,
I threw me down all gasping.

On the mountains mirth, joy upon the earth,
In the river boys were sporting;

But lonely I sat dreamily
My bunch of wild flowers sorting !
My nosegay wild ! More than one lass smiled
To look at these flowers and me, love,
But your hand will take the poor gift for the sake
Of a day I thought on thee, love !

'Tis a humble knot of flowers, I wot,
As might grace a peasant's dwelling ;
Some cornflowers blue, and clover too,
Such as grow each field and dell in ;
Sweet eglantine, and a spray of vine
With its tendrils green to bind them,—
Stuff of little worth—like him who went forth
To meadow and wood to find them !

Flashes fire from his eye, his cheeks flush high,
His hands he clenches trembling,
His heart doth throb, seething hot his blood,
His brow a black cloud resembling ;
His flowers see !—Wretched weeds and he
Despised and forsaken are lying ;
His breast doth heave,—wilt thou pass and leave
Him and them by the wayside dying ?

Freiligrath

A Hamlet on the Rhine[1]

ROMANCE, I greet thee ! Lo, thy eyrie bold !
   Its slender turrets in the air up-towering,
Its crumbling porches, mossy ruins old,
Its castle, firm and rugged to behold,
   How doth it wrap my soul with sway o'erpowering !
Hail, once again ! I tread in pensive dream
Thy fairest refuge on the Rhine's fair stream.

Thou still art here ! In weeds of cloister plain,
   Through coloured panes thou gazest on me sadly,
Outlawed thou art by Reason and her train,
Alas ! the wisdom of this age were fain
   To banish thee for evermore and gladly !
In river strongholds, tottering and decayed,
Thou hidest tremblingly, oh wondrous maid !

In churches, ah, so desolate and bare,
   Yon is the place where loud thy soul is wailing !
In empty churches, thou, with streaming hair,
Dost weeping kneel with many a broken prayer,
   And fervent clinging to the altar's railing,
Within whose shadow's ever sacred calm
Dost seek devout a sanctuary's balm !

[1] Oberwesel.

Yet thou art she, whom oft in days of yore
  A nation's best with rapt delight praised loudly,
Whom Ludwig Tieck's white palfrey ofttimes bore,
Who, through the wood of poesy, before
  Didst dash—Brentano, Arnim following proudly;—
Glows bright the forest, silver-springs around,
And like a dream the Wonder Horn doth sound.

Days long since past!—Adown the shore strode I,
  —Not Volker saw the Rhine more limpid racing—
A steamboat on its way went rushing by,
The wheel ploughed deep, and threw the foam on high,
  Upon the deck one of thy priests was pacing;
The youngest sure—and yet already now
Gray are the locks that float round Uhland's brow!

We recognition waved; my lonely town
  He soon passed by, o'erlooking the swift river;
Upon us twain the Loreley gazed down—
Upon my lips a cry of joy I drown,
  But in my eyes hot tears all trembling quiver;
A mournful song into my memory came,
"Three students crossed the Rhine"—this was its name.

Yes, this the Rhine, whose wave conceals the gold
  Whereon old Uhland's eyes with pleasure glisted!
And yon himself!—Romance, ah! there behold
The inspired lip that truly could unfold
  With magic word, thy glamour an he listed;

Freiligrath

Yon is the eye, that in the enchanted Ring,
Beside the witch-elm, bathed in thy clear spring!

That he was passing—ah! how well you knew!
   From crag and chink, forth through the dewy morning
You gazed on him;—a sunny smile there flew
Just as the vessel turned into my view,
   O'er thy wan features' sad resigned mourning!
With mournful pleasure, thou, on bended knee,
Upon thy river thine own bard didst see!

Yonder he fled, thy youngest, truest knight!
   The last smoke fades in air, the ship retreating;
Gone, too, thy smile; the hills no more stand bright;—
Thy last brave champion that for thee doth fight,—
   And on a steamer!—strange my heart is beating!—
Mediæval inspiration borne away
By a new era's all resistless sway!

A simile! It entered full my soul
   And would not thence again, my will defying!
The melancholy hence that o'er me stole,—
Thou Pale One, hushed and silent be thy dole!
   An iron age 'tis for thee, harsh and trying!
Heedless it undermines thy tottering throne,
Alas, not with its steamer's keel alone!

Thy empire, Lady, has departed long;
   The world has changed; where, now, are thy dominions?

Another spirit than thine rules firm and strong ;
It throbs in life, and flames out into song,
   None e'er before it fluttered thus its pinions !
I also serve and wish it victory glad,—
But why wage war with thee, thou exile sad?

Thou, whose proud banner but from mould'ring wall
   Doth lonely float, through the dull air slow-sailing,
Thou, the Dethroned !—with agitated soul
Down at thy feet, I humbly, sadly fall,
   A solemn witness of thy widow's wailing !
A child, all feverish, of this Era new,
Yet for the Past piously mourning too !

Not as a boy !—Only one hour, lo !
   Stretched at thy feet, I'll join thee in thy sorrow !
The Spirit fresh that through these times doth blow,
I've promised it ; it has my word and vow,
   My blade must flash yet in the fight to-morrow !
Only one hour ! But that devoted quite
To Thee alone, and to thy glory bright.

There, take me to thee, take me in thy hold !
   Hail, battlements, high in the air up-towering !
Hail, crumbling porches, mossy ruins old !
Hail, castle stern ! Thou falcon's eyrie bold !
   How do ye wrap my soul with sway o'erpowering !
Yon doth the Pfalz in fiery sunset shine,
The clouds seem castles—yes ! this land is thine !

Freiligrath

A church !—I enter it as in a dream ;
   The windows, richly stained, are deeply glowing ;
The foliaged pillars throw out haughty gleam,
And through the gloomy cloister's arches dim,
   Careless and wild, a garden small is showing,
Blending its azure and its verdure gay
With the cathedral's ever sombre gray.

And, softly trembling, nods the shadow light
   Of waving boughs, upon the church-wall playing ;
Upon the tomb of Lady and of Knight,
Their figures, carved in marble, stand upright,
   Their hands are raised aloft, as if for praying ;
Gently resigned their pallid faces beam,
The peace of death o'er both doth brightly stream.

A sacred lull !—bustle and trade far gone !—
   Romance, behold, my mourning fast is fleeting !
That joy and peace divine, which is not known
Unto the world, alas !—to thee, alone !
   Here can I feel it in my bosom beating ;
Earth fades away, and Heaven in blissful arms
Enfolds me close,—hushed are the world's alarms !

Enough, enough ! such haven not for aye !
   Back to the Present ! Great is life's attraction !
But what this spot into my heart doth lay
May't flame for ever ! In my pulses may
   It throb unceasing, hallowing every action !

May't give me gladness, strength and courage free,
When the loud day shall hoarsely summon me!

Thus will my service of the Time be pure!
   Oh, exiled maid! with thee I would be grieving;
I came thy shrine to wet with teardrops, sure,
And lo, thou gav'st me power to endure;
   Thy peace doth fill me; calm, behold me leaving!
Thou shed'st thy light around me, I depart—
An exile—but e'en now a Queen thou art!

Farewell, to-day! The sunset's molten gold
   Floods the dim aisle; the deep-toned bells are ringing;
Church banners flutter o'er me half unrolled—
Ye Ever Wise, whom all things must be told,
   Who therefore ask, what now I have been singing?—
Doth glow the eternal lamp, and incense roll—
Call it a Requiem for Brentano's soul!

The Trumpet of Gravelotte [1]

(August, 1870)

DEATH and destruction they belched forth in vain,
   We grimly defied their thunder;
Two columns of foot and batteries twain,
   We rode and cleft them asunder.

---

[1] This poem was suggested by a fact, communicated at the time by the newspapers.

Freiligrath

With brandished sabres, with reins all slack,
    Raised standard and low-couched lances,
Thus we Uhlans and Cuirassiers wildly drove back,
    And fiercely repelled their advances.

But the ride was a ride of death and of blood;
    With our thrusts we forced them to sever,
But of two whole regiments, lusty and good,
    Out of two men one rose never.

With breast shot through, with brow gaping wide,
    They lay stark and cold in the valley,
Snatched away in their youth, in their manhood's pride—
    Now, Trumpeter, sound to the rally!

And he took the trumpet, whose angry thrill
    Urged us on to the glorious battle,
And he blew a blast—but all silent and still
    Was the trump, save a dull hoarse rattle;

Save a voiceless wail, save a cry of woe,
    That burst forth in fitful throbbing—
A bullet had pierced its metal through,
    For the Dead the wounded was sobbing!

For the faithful, the brave, for our brethren all,
    For the Watch on the Rhine, true-hearted!
—Oh, the sound cut into our inmost soul!—
    It brokenly wailed the Departed!

And now fell the night, and we galloped past,
  Watch-fires were flaring and flying,
Our chargers snorted, the rain poured fast—
  And we thought of the dead and the dying.

Emanuel Geibel

In April

O HUMID eve of April,
   How dear to me you are;
The sky is all cloud-curtained,
   With here and there a star.

Like breath of love so balmy
   The air blows warm and wet;
From out the valley rises
   Faint scent of violet.

I fain a song would utter
   That like this eve shall be,
And cannot find so dreamy,
   So soft a melody.

Karl Beck

Resignation

METHOUGHT that already the swallow dreamed
    Of her own true nest;
Methought that already the lark had tried
    The songs in her breast;
Methought that already the blossoms were kissed
    By winds of the west;
Methought that already I held thee clasped,
    Eternally blest.

How winterly have you turned overnight,
    Ye zephyrs mild;
How dead and frozen the blossoms o'ernight
    But yesterday smiled;
How the lark has forgotten overnight
    Her spring-song wild;
And ah, how forgotten overnight
    Thy poor, poor child!

Gottfried Keller

Woodland Songs

I.

STANDS the mighty oaken forest, waving leafy summits hoary,
And to-day, in high good humour, it has sung its old, old story.

First began a tender sapling, gently in the breezes bending,
Then the tempest gathered fury, ever growing, roaring, rending.

Lo, it sweeps in stormy billows, rolling by in solemn gladness;
Raving through the highest branches shrieks the wind aloud in madness.

High o'erhead now howls the tempest, wildly whistling, weirdly moaning;
Deep below, amongst the rootwork, you can hear it creaking, groaning.

Sometimes yells a single oak tree, brandishing its shaft to heaven,
Thundering answer gives the forest, tumult wild of leafy leaven.

Even to a boiling springtide this grand pastime all resembled,
Towards the North the foliage whitened; wind-swept, silver gray it trembled.

Thus, now playing loud, now softly, doth old Pan still strike his lyre,
Teaching all his woods and forests his world-ancient chaunt and quire.

Inexhaustibly he wanders up and down his gamut sweeping,
That in seven tones containeth the world-harmony in its keeping.

And 'neath dripping leaves, young poets and young fledglings cower shrinking,
While in silence they both listen, all the melody in-drinking.

My Bright Eyes are Shining

My bright eyes are shining
Like the heavens afar,
Ride hither and thither,
Thou slim brown Hussar.

Ride hither and thither,
  Then ride back again,
Perhaps it may happen,
  Thou findest thy gain!

Why grazes thy charger
  In my sweet mignonette?
Is that for my true love
  All the thanks that I get?

Thy spurs why entangle
  In my soft spinning yarn?
Why hang thy red jacket
  On the door by the barn?

Sheer off, saucy rider,
  On thy charger so free,
And leave my glad star-eyes
  In peace unto me.

By flowing Waters

I DREAMILY ponder
By the water's soft flow,
And bend my rapt gaze
On the billows below;

I seek—what?—I know not,
In each foam-whitened crest;
Forgotten old visions
Awake in my breast.

Anon, flashes by me
In crystalline clearness,
With lips that are smiling,
In swift sudden nearness,
The World-face familiar,
So ancient and bright!
Its eye rested on me
With heavenly light.

Where has it evanished—
With the billows that rove?
Whence has it descended—
From the welkin above!
For as I gazed upward
Into cloud-drift on high
I just saw it fading
Away in the sky.

I see it most often
When winds are at rest,
And ever its radiance
Expandeth my breast;
But when my soul needeth
Its full presence near,
I see it in storm, too,
Distinctly and clear.

Winter Night

Not a wing beat through the frozen air,
Calm and silent lay the dazzling snow,
Not a cloud hung on the night-sky fair,
Not a wave stirred the numb lake below.

From its depth arose the coral-tree
Till its summit touched the ice and froze;
Climbing up upon its branches free,
Gazing upwards still, the Nixie rose.

And I stood upon the fragile glass
Which divided that black gulf from me,
Close, close under foot I saw her pass,
Her white beauty limb by limb did see.

And with stifled moan she gropes along
That hard roof, all green and crystalline;
Never, never shall I cease to long
For that sweet dark face so close to mine!

Klaus Groth

"He talked, oh so much"

He talked, oh so much, but not yes and not no
I replied, all I said was : "Now, John, I must go!"

He talked both of heaven and earth and his love,
He talked—I scarce know now what things he talked of.

He talked, oh so much, but not yes and not no
I replied, all I said was : "Now, John, I must go!"

He held fast my hand ; with a tear in his eye
He asked could I love him, and would I not try?

Though not angry, I said not a word, yes or no,
And all that I said was : "Now, John, I must go!"

And now sitting thinking, my thoughts will run on,
That I ought to have said : "Ah, how joyfully, John!"

Yet, came he to-morrow—not yes and not no
Would I answer, but only : "Now, John, I must go."

FOLK LORE

Old Büsum

In the wild Haff lies Büsum brave,
The tide crept up and delved a grave.

The stealthy tide crept sure and slow,
Till it had gnawed the island through.

No fence remained, nor stick nor stone,
The waves washed all remorseless down.

Nor dog nor beast again gave sound,
They all lie deep on ocean's ground.

And all who lived and laughed in light,
The sea has covered with black night.

Whiles, when the tide is very low,
Sometimes the tops of houses show.

A church spire points from out the sand,
As 'twere the finger of a hand.

Then you may hear the bells soft ringing,
Then you may hear a soft sad singing;

Then you may hear a hushed low cry:
"Bury our limbs in earth on high."

"He woke"

She entered softly in her shroud and held a burning light,
She was still paler than her shroud and as the wall so white.

Thus came she slowly towards the bed, the curtains drew away,
She held the candle to his face and bent down where he lay.

Her mouth and eyes were firmly closed, the lashes touched her cheek,
No limb she moved and yet she looked as one who fain would speak.

Cold terror crept along his back and froze his blood and bone,
He thought to shriek in deadly fear, but lo, his voice was gone.

He thought to seize it with his hands, the spectre cold and mute,
And felt in all his agony, he stirred nor hand nor foot.

And when he woke from out his trance, she went out by the door,
As pale as death, in graveyard shroud, holding the light before.

Groth

The Haunted Moor

What moans so loud in moor and bush?
Sure 'tis the wind in reed and rush;
'Tis neither reed nor nightwind's sigh,
'Tis woman's moan and infant's cry.

You hear it wailing weak and ill,
All night you hear it sobbing still;
But ere the morning sun comes round
It sinks like mist into the ground.

And when the shepherd sleeps at noon,
He hears a distant muffled croon,
So deep, so hollow, soft and low,
As mother hushed her child below.

It is a restless soul, they say,
That flies at morning's streak away;
It is a soul whose peace is gone,
That sadly thus doth make its moan.

And when the moor is bleak and bare,
And autumn leaves whirl through the air,
Then flies, 'midst all the uproar wild,
A death-pale maiden with her child.

Upon yon heath there is a moor,
There willows grow but scant and poor;

Upon yon heath a pool lies drear,
There neither frog nor toad you hear.

The white sheepgrass grows all around,
Its depth no man as yet did sound ;
Its water sickers green and slow,
And only breaks whiles further through.

That is the place she threw it in,
Now she must haunt it for its sin ;
She stands and wild her locks doth tear,
Then she is gone until next year.

Autumn is near, the quail doth cry,
The cuckoo long hath said good-bye ;—
Listen, how loud the moans and clear,
'Twill soon be silent till next year.

The Haunted House

By day it looks a cheerful house, with panes and windows
    bright,
But soon as twilight dim sets in, 'tis eerie then by night.

Then someone steals on slippers soft down passage and
    by door,
But when at length the morning dawns, the sound is heard no
    more.

Groth

'Tis just as if a woman old were looking all the night
For something that she could not find, and searched till morning's light.

From out the parlour it comes forth and wanders all about,
It tries each door and feels each lock, as though the key were out.

It fumbles at the kitchen door, it gently lifts the latch,
And feels its darkling way about with many a grope and scratch.

Then on it shuffles 'gainst the wall, and rustles as it goes,
And now the stairs begin to creak beneath the ghostly toes.

And in the lumber attic next doth rummage without end,
Till slams the door with muffled sound,—again it doth descend.

The large room hath an iron chain, 'tis clanked whole hours they say—
But all doth vanish when the cock doth crow at break of day.

The Holy Oak

THERE stands a tree the churchyard by, close to the winding brook,
The village boys climb every tree, but never climb this oak.

A gnarled old trunk it stands alone, all twisted and awry,
One branch, like to a threatening arm, it stretches to the sky.

The village boys climb every tree, but this old oak they shun,
At night it threatens with its arm and awes the noisiest one.

At night it threatens with its arm, and strikes them dumb with fear,
Then neither child nor woman goes alone the churchyard near.

The birds they fly in every tree, light flitting to and fro,
Here not a sparrow will alight, nor even owl or crow.

High on the top dost rock a nest, 'tis never left, they say,
A coal-black raven sits within, and screams by night and day.

He screams so hollow all the year, his voice is hoarse and harsh,
He thus has screamed as long as men have lived upon the marsh.

'Tis said he'll scream a hundred years, then fly to North away,
Then will a mighty branch shoot forth from the old oak, they say:

Then will another bird come down, with wings all white to see,
And build its nest upon the oak, then will the good time be:

Then birds will seek the oak again, then boys will romp and climb,
Then will the old folk rest beneath, in that good coming time.

The raven screams, the tree stands dark, the leaves whirl from the bough—
Methinks 'twill ever stand as grim, as desolate as now.

The Knotted Stick

He had a stout old walking stick, a blackthorn strong, I wot,
'Twas tipped with ferrule bright of brass, a nail in every knot.

With staff of oak and Spanish cane it stood behind the door,
And when it raps, he forth must wend, far over fell and moor.

Then he turns pale, his mother weeps, and earnestly doth pray,
But though she pray and though she weep, at home he may not stay.

He takes the stick from out its nook, his face of ashen hue,
He takes his hat, no word doth speak, and wanders all night through.

And whether he doth sit at meals, or whether he doth sleep,
Ay, though he slept the sleep of death, 'twould break that slumber deep.

Then he must rise in dreary night and grope behind the door,
And wander with his stick alone o'er fell and snowy moor.

His mother lies awake and weeps, but ere the farm cock crows,
He doth return, as pale as death, as from the grave he rose.

Then he doth neither eat nor drink, but lies in stupor dead;
Then silently works on again, till the next summons dread.

And when he's called he cannot rest, but he must straight away,
But always he returns again before the break of day.

Where doth he go? He never says, nor what he sees doth tell,
But he doth know each funeral round, ere tolls the passing bell.

They say, as soon as the last month of any man has run,
He must away, if he walk miles, till he has found that one.

And that, on gazing through the panes, as corpse in shroud doth see,
Who with his children yet doth romp perchance in careless glee.

Then at the window taps he thrice, peering with glassy stare,
Full many a heart has given a bound and spinning-wheel stopped there.

Groth

Full many a heart has jumped with fright, when on the shutters low,
His rap is heard, one, two, and three; and then his face doth show.

Then is he gone! And now, they say, he meets the funeral slow,
Then must he fly right o'er their heads, high through the air must go.

High over heads and shoulders all, high o'er the coffin too,
Then must he watch them passing on where grows the churchyard yew.

Then has he neither peace nor rest till tolls the passing bell,
And he has seen the funeral train a second time as well.

With clouded cane and oaken staff the stick stands by the door,
And when it raps he forth must wend, far over fell and moor.

He's thrown it down a quarry deep, he's thrown it in the brook,
But when he opes his parlour door, the stick stood in its nook.

He's fiercely broken it in twain, he's chopped it o'er and o'er,
Arrived at home, the stick was safe behind the parlour door.

He burned it—there it was again; he lost it, back it came,
And burning, losing, chopping it, the stick was there the same.

One day, 'twas just on Christmas-eve, a man came to the door,
He went and fetched the knotted stick, and it was seen no more.

Hans Iwer

His land lies waste and drear his cot;
His soul has peace at last, God wot.

Hans Iwer all betimes doth rouse:
"Get up! get up! and milk the cows!"

The girl doth start with fright and fear:
"Coming, Hans Iwer! yes, I hear!"

She was an orphan without friends,
She says her prayers ere she descends.

Her kirtle's thin, her skirt is spare,
She throws a kerchief o'er her hair.

She tucks her gown unto her knee,
She takes her pails and forth goes she.

So young and weary still is she,
And tottering tremble foot and knee.

Groth

The grass with dew is wet and chill,
The meadows lie so gray and still.

And then—she knows not how or when,
But terror cold chills every vein.

Is it a fox darts o'er the way?
Is it a dog doth bark and bay?

She seems to hear Hans Iwer call:
"Get up and milk the cows withal!"

She springs aside all in her fear,
Good God! a wolf is standing there!

Shrouded in mist he barks and growls,
The wide field echoes with his howls.

Then, shaking like an aspen bough,
She cries: "Hans Iwer! Coming now!"

And when her fright had passed away,
The wolf had vanished, broke the day.

She milked her cows and home she sped,
Sick lay Hans Iwer on his bed.

That night he died, alone, in pain,
No man the werewolf saw again.

His soul has peace at last, God wot,
But waste and lone lie land and cot.

Hermann Lingg

The Black Death

TREMBLE, oh world ! The Plague am I,
Through all the lands I'm going,
Preparing me a banquet high,
Fever is lurking in mine eye,
And black my cloak is flowing.

I come from Egypt's sultry land,
In lurid mists red-veiling,—
From Nile's fen-swamps, from murky strand,
From dragons' spawn in burning sand
Rank poisonous germs inhaling.

I reap, I mow, I stretch my stave
O'er mountain range and billow ;
I'm laying waste the world so brave,
Before each house I plant a grave,
And eke a weeping willow.

Lingg

I am mankind's Destroyer dread,
I'm Death the grim, the awful;
Drought stalks before me, gaunt of tread,
At famine price I sell the bread,
To war the heir I'm lawful.

It matters not how far you hie,
I stride with stride yet wider;
Swift-footed, the Black Plague am I,
The swiftest vessel I o'erfly,
Outride the fastest rider.

The merchant in his merchandise,
Home bears me to his dwelling;
He gives a feast with sparkling eyes,—
Forth from his wealth I ghastly rise,
And on the bier I fell him.

No castled rock so steeply hung,
To me it must surrender;
No pulse doth beat for me too strong,
No body is for me too young,
No heart for me too tender.

Whose eyes my withering eyes infest,
He cares for day no longer;
Whose board, or meat or wine, I've blessed.
He thirsts alone for rest, for rest,
For dust alone doth hunger.

In Asia died the mighty Chan,—
Where Cinnamon Isles are shining;
Died Negro Prince and Mussulman;
Nightly you hear at Ispahan
The dogs round carrion whining.

Byzantium was a blooming town,
And Venice smiled in beauty,
Now, like dead leaf, their hosts sink down,
And who collects the foliage brown,
Will soon be quit his duty.

Where Norway's farthest cliffs rise white,
Into some port forsaken,
I cast a vessel empty quite,
And all on whom I breathed my blight,
Must slumber ne'er to waken.

They're strewn and scattered everywhere,
Though days and months be flying;
No soul to count the hours hath care;—
Years hence, you'll silent find and bare,
Death's City lonely lying.

Moritz Hartmann

Bulgarian Lament

ARE they roses, are they red, red blossoms,
That so thickly fill our homestead's valley?
Are they clouds of brown and white wood-pigeon,
That fly circling round yon mountain summit?
Ah, not roses they, in sooth, nor blossoms,
Flames are they, red licking flames, and lurid,
That so thickly fill our homestead's valley,
And not clouds of brown and white wood pigeon
Which encircle yonder mountain summit;
Smoke it is, dense smoke, opaque and rolling,
For our lone deserted huts are burning.

On the mountain side we roam as vagrants,
Hide behind the bushes e'en as Heyducs,
Huddling close like sheep all lost and straying.
Cursed be they who set on fire our houses,
Be they Muscovite, or be they Turkish,

Be they Christian, ay, or be they heathen!
May God's direst curses now befall them,
Or the devil's best and choicest blessing!
May they drown by thousands in the Danube,
Stopping up and damming her blue billows,
As they desolated our poor country.
May wild Varna's breakers cast ashore them,
And there leave them, black and rotting corpses,
That the very air may steam corruption.

Out, alas! What now will say our pilgrims,
Who within Jerusalem are resting,
Kissing there our Saviour's feet, the golden,
When they shall return and find their houses
Wasted all and burnt, and naught but ashes?
When they shall return with pictures beauteous
Of our saints, which they have purchased yonder,
Painted gay in colours, rolled on rollers,
And shall then, alas, a wall find never
Whereupon to hang the beauteous pictures?

Vast our country is, vast and unending,
Who shall tell us, *where* in days of future—
Who shall tell us, *if* in days of future—
Our poor huts again shall be rebuilded?
Fortune, ah, it grows not quick as rye grows,
Grows not by the road as humble weeds do,
And not like the dear sun sets it ever,
Only to rise bravely on the morrow.

Hartmann

Slow grows fortune, like unto old tree stems,
Slowly, slowly, if again, perhaps, ever.
With the lead inside flies yet the falcon,
With our sorrow we yet wander onward.

Let this year dread winter not come on us,
Let it not, oh Heaven, full of mercy!
Banish it behind thy clouds of darkness,
That we may not stiffen in the forests,
In the bitter wind-tossed winter forests!
For no home this year have our poor children,
And no home have our poor wives and mothers;
Listen, how they weep and wail in anguish:
Lo, nor home nor roof possess our husbands!

Nothing saved, except the coins of silver
Which our dear fair maidens always carry
On their necks, instead of necklets costly;
Give to us those coins of fair white silver,
Give them us, ye fair and gracious maidens,
That we may buy bread to give our children!

Take them all, our coins of fair white silver,
But no bread is to be found, oh sorrow,
In the land, not e'en for golden ducats,—
Sad our stricken country, sad and dreary.

Victor von Scheffel

Heini of Steier

The Nightingale calls to the Finches' gay brood :
" A fiddle is ringing sweet-toned through the wood ;
Ye twitterers and chatterers, oh, hush now your strain,
For Heini of Steier has come back again ! "

The old village cobbler his cap waves with glee :
" Now Heaven in its mercy remembereth me !
Sole-leather will rise and dance-shoone burst in twain,
Now Heini of Steier has come back again ! "

To the dance are fast flocking, with frolic and jest,
The maids crowned with chaplets, arrayed in their best :
" Where tarry the suitors ? Our hearts are all fain . . .
For Heini of Steier has come back again ! "

And who dons her kirtle for frisking it gay ?
'Tis old wrinkled granny, waxing young, too, to-day ;
Lean-legged, like a heron, she stalks down the lane . . .
Faith, Heini of Steier has come back again !

Scheffel

His flock leaves the shepherd all heedless behind,
Leaves the peasant his plough and his horses the hind,
The farmer and bailiff chide loudly in vain:
"That Heini of Steier has come back again!"

But he takes, all silent, his fiddle to hand,
Half brooding, half playing, unconscious doth stand.
Chords gush forth electric, like soft fiery rain . . .
Lo! Heini of Steier has come back again.

. . . In the nuns' cloister garden, on flowery steep,
Bends one o'er the fountain, and listening doth weep:
"Oh veil, oh black raiment, oh bitterest pain,
My Heini of Steier has come back again!"

Paul Heyse

The Valley of the Espingo

They marched o'er the mountains, following the stream,
Moorish soldiery, mounted and bold ;
To fight with the Franks was their eager dream,
In troops they marched by each swollen stream,
Where the snows of the Pyrenees melted cold.

Through the humid ravine wave their mantles murk,
Keen blows the blast from the peaks on high ;
Their eyes search around, threaten lance and dirk,
No Basque plumed bonnet unseen may lurk—
And the dread Basque arrows, how swift they fly !

Wearily thus the whole day they wend,
Dreary the path, hasty the ride ;
Endless the pine-woods seem to extend,
The mule needs the lash ere the journey's end,
And the snorting charger slackens his stride.

Heuse

Suddenly, lo, from the gorges wild,
Falling abruptly, down leads the way;
And they gaze on a scene delightful and mild,
Fair meadows bordering on mountains piled,
Butterflies soaring in sunset ray.

How verdant the mead, and how balmy the air,
Boughs scarce tremble, so tenderly kissed,
The orange blooms and the jonquil fair,
Sweet red roses blush everywhere,
All lies bathed in a sunny mist.

And the Moors are touched by the wondrous spell,
Dear past days in memory they see,
When they hunted the Hauran's swift gazelle,
When they listened to love and roamed the dell,
And plucked the roses of Engadi.

And with joy they descend, and the host scatters wide,
Zephyrs tenderly fan their hot brow;
As round Bagdad's rose-plains in fragrant pride,
Where the ocean tempers the fierce noontide,
So the lake wafts humid moisture now.

Their anxious fears how quickly they go,
Weapons and arms are cast aside;
They wander in rapture where roses blow,
Their hearts as with meeting sweetly aglow,
And they dip to bathe in the limpid tide.

Ah, home! ah, bliss! To their laughter and glee,
The watch within list with envy sore.
So peaceful the fair earth seems to be,
They are tempted to roam o'er the fragrant lea,
And those who should watch, they watch no more.

They watch no longer! But Night's fell breed,
Treachery watches, secret and sly!
It steals from the forest with silent speed,
It creeps to the tents: have heed, have heed!
The dread Basque arrows, how fast they fly!

Too late, too near is the danger at hand!
Weaponless, they, amid roses' breath,
All are cut down, each valiant band;
Ah, treacherous dream, so seductive and bland,
Ah, image of Home, thou broughtest Death.

Robert Hamerling

The Incantation of the Dead

(From "Ahasuerus")

At midnight hour, in lonely chamber drear,
Vaulted, cavernous, dead and windowless,
(Having regard not to the outward world,
But turned within, as is the soulless eye
Of one in slumber—) broods the Necromant.
Silent he sits and still, while lurid lamps
Pour down a flickering and uncertain light
On strange dread instruments. With stolid stare
Gaze from the walls Egyptian images
In human-bestial shape: Bubastis, see,
And Horus, Typhon, Isis and Osiris;
And ever in between creep mystic signs,
Like reptiles crawling up and down the walls.
On lofty pedestals gleam metal mirrors,
Funereal urns with ashes of the dead,

And black-charred bones.—Still more receptacles
Hold deadly herbs, while yonder, lo, doth hang
A human skeleton, and overhead
Hangs a dead raven. Here doth lie extended
An alligator; yonder, heads of dog,
Of sparrow-hawk and of the holy Ibis.
Here gloats a lifeless lynx; there, glassy-eyed
A dead hyæna stares.—Breathes not one spark
Of life beneath this dry rot and decay?
Ay, but there does!—Crouched at the Wizard's feet
A black dog growls and snarls, as though he were
Twin brother to the dog of Hecate;
A tawny snake glides tortuous, in smooth coils,
Across the room with red unwinking eyes;
While in yon corner squats a venomous toad,
Bloated of bulk.
    The Necromant doth brood
Deep wrapt in thought. From Egypt hath he come,
From the old sacred country of the Dead,
Whose glory now decays. In wanton Rome,
Where life in joyous billows surges high,
All lonely stands the Wanderer from the Nile,
As were he messenger of Death. Deep glowing
Flashes within the eye of this Magician
That mystic light, born of the Orient,
Which ever but in smouldering blazes forth
Its fire into our cool gray Occident.
But quietly soon shall draw near the day
(—'Tis promised by this man's dark flashing eye!—)

When from the East triumphantly shall break
A fuller stream of this same dazzling light,
Gathering the nations of the western world
Together to a worship new and strange !
Thoughts, world-transforming, glow and seethe beneath
The bronzed and dark-haired brows of earnest thinkers,
From Libyan shore or from Judæan strand.
Forerunners of an Era new, these men
From Egypt and Chaldæa walk the world,
Soothsayers they and Seers, Tellers of dreams;
And this same shining mystic glow of thought
Rests on the brow of Apollonius too.
Driven by unrest, he came to Rome and heard
With smile of scorn that Nero boasted proudly
Of his omnipotence.—" Can *he* subdue
Spirits and Hell itself? Not he, in faith,
But Apollonius can."
      To him hath come
An old man, sad-eyed and mysterious,
Who more than once had urged him to arouse
And furnish him with all his occult might
To do a deed of dread and awful glamour,
The object, sooth, to put to shame a Nero !

When Apollonius from his brooding dreams
At length looks up, behold, there stands before him
This stranger old, sad-eyed, mysterious,
A rapid word is whispered 'twixt the twain,
And then the other silently conducts

Into the dusky room of the Magician,
Rome's mighty Ruler.
                    "Art thou he," quoth Nero,
"To whom is given secret might to compel
The Dead to rise up from the shades of Hades?"
"Not only these I govern, Imperator,
The very demons bow to my behest,
Bound by the secret laws of occult powers;
And e'en the gods on high obey my will,
For firm resolve *is* magic—*is* the godhead."

"*Such is my creed!*—But if to me thou'lt prove
That *thy* volition yet the will of Nero
Transcends in occult and mysterious skill,
Then open unto me the gates of Hades,
And bring before mine eyes dead Agrippina!"

The other's quiet answer: "I can do it."
And then he pours with gloomy eye intent
O'er signs obscure and cabalistic scrolls
That he may find in tablets cuneiform
Th' auspicious moment. Then, on glowing brasiers
He incense throws, whence, in white vap'rous wreaths,
Rises a subtle odour. Lamps, strange fashioned,
Stand upon brackets and on pillars quaint,
Shedding across the fumes a blood-red light.
And now the Wizard reaches down dark herbs,
White Asphodel, Vervain and Aconite,

Hamerling

Potent of spell and succulent, all cut
With brazen sickle on the Pontine shore.

Meanwhile, half in derision smiling, Nero
Glances around the chamber, when his eye
Falls on a polished mirror, burnished brightly;
Whence meets his gaze, in jeering merriment,
A hideous face, more scoffing than his own.
Swift he recoils, and seemingly irate
The Wizard hastens up and throws a veil
Across the mirror's bright and tell-tale surface.

Then he lifts up a stone from out the floor,
And slaughters o'er the gaping aperture
A black lamb to the powers of dread Avernus;
Then, murmuring mystic words, he lets the stream
Hot trickle down into the earth below.
The dog slinks up to lick the moisture warm,
But the Magician drives him off with blows,
Until he seeks a distant corner howling.

The steam of blood now rises. Apollonius
Catches within a bowl some of the ichor,
And then lets fall three measured drops of blood
Within a goblet, foaming rich and sweet,
Which now he hands to Nero that he taste it.
The rest he sprinkles, muttering, drop by drop;
And, lo, wherever such a drop alights
There straight awakes a strange and awful life,

Born of the brasiers' steaming exhalations,
Born of the weird red flickering of the lamps,
Born of strange sounds and spirit-tones that seem
Wafted from vast and awful space.—Things dead
Stir with a ghostly life.
The eyes of the dead lynx, the dead hyæna,
'Gin suddenly to glitter fierce and bright,
Their nostrils twitch, as lustful to inhale
The welcome steam of blood; the lifeless raven
Hanging above the grisly skeleton
Flutters its wings first slow, then faster, stronger,
And digs its beak into the bony framework
That now appears to clothe itself in flesh,
And softly to moan out in gnawing pain.
The alligator opes his bristling maw,
A cloud of owls and bats wheel round and flutter
Athwart the room with soft and spectral wings.

The Necromant, still pacing through the room,
Sprinkles bright drops on this side and on that;
And now, against his will, a drop alights
In one of those bronze talismanic urns,
Wherein lie bones and ashes of the dead.
Up from the ashes flamelets leap and hiss,
And from the urn doth rise a pallid head,
A death-pale face, with eyes all firmly shut.
Enraged, the Wizard rushes to the spot,
And presses back with quick and trembling hands,
The apparition dread into the urn.

Hamerling

And now their wings attempt the sparrow-hawks,
And fluttering scream and fly across the room;
But at their screeching waxes wrath the toad,
Furious the crocodile, the yellow serpent;
In turmoil wild they hiss and yelp and snarl,
A wailing as of wind goes through the air,
And in between, a moaning, sobbing, barking,
As noise of waters, howling fierce of tempest.
The black dog mingles in the creatures' strife
With furious madness; foaming rears the snake,
The toad spirts wildly round its venom black.
The Wizard, ever muttering spells, collects
The flecks of foam from off the dog's white fangs,
The serpent's slaver and the toad's foul venom,
Mixing it all, with henbane leaves thrown in,
Within the smoking pool of blood below.

But wilder, madder yet, more clamorous rises
The furious racket of the spectral rabble.
Nero, aghast, lifts up his foot to crush
The serpent's head that madly darts at him;
When, wilder still than all the previous uproar,
A Stygian tempest rushes through the house,
Whose thundering roar is blent with groans of death.
The earth doth quake, and goblins mow and dance
With gibbering ghosts; the very gods of Memphis,
Dog and bird-headed, join the unholy revels.

Into this weird and furious whirl of spectres,
Into this brood of Hell, now broken loose,

The Wizard suddenly calls, loud and clear,
A single mystic and commanding word ;
And in an instant vanishes the rabble
To Stygian shades, and all the hideous uproar.

An odour, sweet and faint of violets,
Steals o'er the senses ; and a purple glow
Enshrouds the distance, whence, in rosy cloud
Approaching nearer—look you, where she comes !—
With features sweet and pale, with garlands crowned
Of lilies, violets and asphodel,
Her eyes firm closed,—floats hither Agrippina !

Emil Rittershaus

On the Battlefields of Metz

(September, 1870)

O'ER fields crushed down and trodden
My foot passed, sad and slow;
Those who grim death have suffered
Now stilly rest below.
The greensward, drenched and sodden
With noble blood and brave,
Now yields unto the fighters
A solemn quiet grave.

Here lie, without or coffin
Or winding sheet and shroud,
Who stood upon this mountain,
The battle raging loud;
A cross of withered branches
Is all the graves can show,
What doth the inscription tell me:
"Two hundred sleep below!"

And further yet and onwards,
What do these tablets say?
By thousands rest dead warriors
Laid low in earth and clay;
Of arms and shells, the splinters
Thick o'er the grass are strewn—
Oh, grimly Death the Reaper
On that stern day hath mown!

Each blade of grass is weeping,
Cold drops cling far and nigh,
While o'er the meadows sweeping
I hear low requiems sigh;
Discordant rises yonder
Of ravens black a cloud,
And dense white mists are weaving
O'er all a giant shroud.

And they, who fought so bravely,
For ever now shall sleep
Here in the yellow cornfields,
Or by yon vineyards steep;
And when spring airs shall softly
Wander o'er field and plain,
Then o'er these mounds the peasant
Shall drive his plough again.

Where you, oh noble comrades,
Your final home have found,

Rittershaus

The corn shall sprout yet higher
A foot above the ground ;
The dead men in the vineyards
To the roots give lusty life,
The yellow and blue clusters
With twofold strength are rife !

Ye, who the foe sank fighting,
Ye men and striplings true,
We've buried you, and sadly
Our soul doth weep for you !
Your last dread hour has sounded,
Your work is done—ye sleep,
E'en as the mighty rootwork
Of trees imbedded deep.

From North and South together
The time called loudly Ye ;
You are the roots and fibres
Of the Tree of Unity !
Lo, North and South are clasping
Their hands with fervent strain—
Nought forges hearts together
So firm as grief and pain.

As, when the bullets whistled,
Hot anger made us one—
Now shall the golden crops of Peace
For all ripe in the sun !

We've stood in flames and flashes,
With weapons keen and bright—
Now shall the fiery vintage
Of freedom us delight.

Lo, if our crops grow verdant
O'er German field and dale,
We owe it you, ye brave ones,
Ye silent men and pale!
And if on German vinestems
The grape hangs ripe to-day,
You've paid it with your heartblood.
Oh, bitter price to pay!

When hushed the battle thunders,
Your Nation proud will write
Your names in golden letters
On bronze and marble white,
But Time may mar the marble,
Crumbling to dross the ore—
In the memory of your nation
Ye live for evermore.

Rittershaus

"I asked the sun"

I ASKED the sun: "Say, what is love, ah tell me?"
He gave no answer, only rays of gold;
I asked the flowers: "What is love, ah tell me?"
They shed sweet perfume, but no answer told.

I asked the Almighty: "What is love? or holy,
Or frivolous? To know I would be fain!"
Then God gave me a loved and faithful woman,
And never asked I what was love again.

Felix Dahn

Kriemhild

From her balcony Queen Kriemhild o'er the burnished heather spied,
Shields she saw and sheen of helmets flashing from the mountain side.

From her brow her gold-red tresses back she pushes with white hand :
"Welcome now, my guests of Bergund, welcome to Queen Kriemhild's land.

"Seven years full sorely, sorely, have I yearned to see this day,
Grievously was tried my patience, slow the hours crept on their way.

"When yon Hun's abhorred kisses I with secret loathing bore,
For this hour which now is striking have I waited evermore.

"Now thy weapons seize, King Etzel, called by men the
  Scourge of God,
Now shalt thou my dowry furnish burning fierce in flame and
  blood.

"Not in vain I gave my body to the greatest king of war,
For revenge, revenge shall soothe me, as no woman had
  before!

"At my drawbridge, see, King Gunther, wildly rears thy
  charger back!
Vainly dost thou hush and soothe him, never shall he bear
  thee back!

"When my Siegfried rode out hunting, nought of danger
  dreaded he,
Yet didst thou so foully slay him, who so fondly trusted
  thee.

"Who is that? Not Hagen, surely? Blinded by the Gods, I
  ween,
Would he else have dared to venture where Kriemhilda
  reigns as queen!

"Though thy head rise ne'er so proudly, towering over friend
  and foe,
That on Siegfried's heart has rested this my hand shall
  smite it low!

"But on yonder milkwhite palfrey, with his gold locks waving wild,
He with sunny smile and gentle, that is Giselher the child.

"Woe, my brother, bright and courteous, with thy cheeks a tender red,
Woe, that thou to Kriemhild's banquet, with the others forth hast sped.

"Look ye, they have all dismounted, Hagen too ! with sullen fall,
Clangs the brazen gate behind them—mine, yes mine, are all, are all!"

Hagen's Death Song

Now I'm the last remaining, the princes all are dead,
How in the silver moonlight the bloodstained floor shines red !

My jovial glad Burgundians, how quiet are they now,
I hear their heart-blood trickling from open gashes slow.

Up from the palace rises a steam and smell of blood,
And for their meal hoarse shrieking, the vultures leave the wood.

Dahn

King Gunther tosses wildly with fever dreams oppressed,
Since a sharp bolt descending, cleft keen his helmet's crest.

Slain lies the tuneful Volcker—he laughed out as he died:
"Take all I have, oh Hagen, my fiddle take!" he cried.

To guard from Hunnish treason, his fiddle dear to screen,
He bore it on his trusty back which never foe hath seen.

Like nightingale it sounded when Volcker bent the bow,—
Far differently 'twill echo in my rough hands, I trow!

Four strings, I see, are broken—three whole ones yet I spy,
I never yet have twirled them, no fiddler sweet am I;—

To-day I fain am tempted to list grim Hagen's lay,
An honest heartfelt cursing's as good as prayer, I say!

So now I curse all women—Woman what's false and base:
Lo, for two white-limbed women must die Burgundian race!

Out on the weak illusion of love and such like prate,
All love is but a fiction and real is only hate!

Fools but repent their action!—That is but worthy of breath,
With sword in hand, hot hate in heart, proud to endure till death.

Had I to shape my life anew, my actions one by one,
'Fore Heaven, there's not a single deed that I should wish undone.

And were a second Siegfried, beloved of men, to appear,
Again I'd thrust into his back a second time my spear!

Why snap, ye craven lute-strings? Do ye refuse such song?
Hark, who with step of thunder the palace stalks along.

And nearer yet and nearer—a shadow grim and great—
This is no Hunnish slave or spy, this sounds like march of
    fate!

Up and arouse, King Gunther!—I know that stride so
    stern,—
Up and arouse, 'tis Death, Revenge! Lo, Dietrich comes,
    of Berne!

Heinrich Vierordt

Cupid's Market

BECAUSE all lone and sad my house,
I went to Cupid's market near,
To buy myself a little god.

The woman offered me thereon
A nestful of the dainty ware,
In gilded basket, latticed o'er.

But I said : nay, it is enough,
Good woman, one love is enough—
And so I chose my little rogue.

Then seized she roughly with her hand
One of the cupids by his wings,
And handed me the wailing boy.

Ah, gently, my good woman, soft,
Lest you should hurt his tender plumes,
For delicate are these same goods !

With shy arch eyes the baby boy
Twinkled his thanks all gratefully,
And silvery bright his voice laughed out.

I took the baby home with me,
And gave it for a home my heart,
And fed it like a little bird.

By day he points his arrows keen,
At night he lights his little lamp,
To light me to some silent tryst.

No longer sad and lone my house.

Dioscuri

My path led by the blue salt bay,
Rocks on the right, to left the sea,
Fiercely the noontide sun beat down,
Glittered each grain of shining sand.

All lost in dreams I wandered on
Along the cragged and rocky beach,
When suddenly I heard the snort
Of horses near, and stood transfixed.

From gleaming sea-foam rose to view
Two splendid chargers black as night;

Vierorbt

Their withers cleaved the limpid wave,
And billows rippled round their flanks.

All stirrupless and saddleless,
Their arching necks flung proudly back,
Thus rambled they along the beach,
And joyfully their neighs rang out.

A stripling youth bestrode each horse,
Features and shoulders as of bronze,
But breast and thigh as marble white,
In glorious god-like nakedness.

Are ye the Dioscuri, say,
Those brother charioteers of Rome?
Did you desert your centuries' watch
By Fountain and by Quirinal?

Nought in creation may surpass
In fiery strength and lusty pride,
In youthful glad exuberance—
On naked steed the naked man!

The breakers that ran dripping off,
Played round, and lit up shimmering
Their bodies as with silver sheen,
E'en as they were Olympus' gods!

CHISWICK PRESS:—CHARLES WHITTINGHAM AND CO.
TOOKS COURT, CHANCERY LANE, LONDON.

A Selection

FROM

MR. WM. HEINEMANN'S LIST

REMBRANDT: His Life, His Work, and His Time. By ÉMILE MICHEL. Translated by FLORENCE SIMMONDS. Edited and prefaced by FREDERICK WEDMORE. With 67 Plates and 250 Illustrations in the Text. 2 vols., royal 8vo, £2 2s. net. Also an Edition on Japanese paper, limited to 150 Copies. Price on application.

A FRIEND OF THE QUEEN. MARIE ANTOINETTE AND COUNT FERSEN. By PAUL GAULOT. Translated from the French by Mrs. CASHEL HOEY. In 2 vols., 8vo. With 2 Portraits. Price 24s.

THE ROMANCE OF AN EMPRESS. CATHERINE II. OF RUSSIA. By R. WALISZEWSKI. Translated from the French. Second Edition. 8vo. With Portrait. Price 7s. 6d.

MEMOIRS. By CHARLES GODFREY LELAND (HANS BREITMANN). Second Edition. 8vo. With Portrait. Price 7s. 6d.

VILLIERS DE L'ISLE ADAM: His Life and Works. From the French of VICOMTE ROBERT DU PONTAVICE DE HEUSSEY. By LADY MARY LOYD. With Portrait and Facsimile. Crown 8vo, cloth, 10s. 6d.

ALFRED, LORD TENNYSON. A Study of His Life and Work. By ARTHUR WAUGH, B.A. Oxon. With 5 Portraits, and 20 Illustrations from Photographs specially taken for this work. New Edition. Crown 8vo, cloth, 7s. 6d.

TWENTY-FIVE YEARS IN THE SECRET SERVICE. The Recollections of a Spy. By Major LE CARON. In One Volume, 8vo. With Portraits and Facsimiles. 14s. Also Popular Edition, crown 8vo, boards, 2s. 6d., cloth, 3s. 6d.

THE GREAT WAR OF 189-. A Forecast. By Rear-Admiral COLOMB, Col. MAURICE, R.A., Major HENDERSON, Staff College, Captain MAUDE, ARCHIBALD FORBES, CHARLES LOWE, D. CHRISTIE MURRAY, F. SCUDAMORE, and Sir CHARLES DILKE. In 1 vol., 8vo, illustrated. 12s. 6d.

LOVE SONGS OF ENGLISH POETS, 1500–1800. With Notes by RALPH H. CAINE. Fcap. 8vo, cloth extra, 3s. 6d.
⁂ Also 100 Copies printed on Hand-made paper, 10s. 6d. net.

GOSSIP IN A LIBRARY. By EDMUND GOSSE. Second Edition. Crown 8vo, gilt top, 7s. 6d.
⁂ Large Paper Edition, limited to 100 copies. Price 25s. net.

QUESTIONS AT ISSUE. Essays. By EDMUND GOSSE. Crown 8vo, buckram, gilt top, 7s. 6d.
⁂ A Limited Edition on Large Paper, 25s. net.

THE ROSE: A Treatise on the Cultivation, History, Family Characteristics, &c., of the Various Groups of Roses. With Accurate Description of the Varieties now Generally Grown. By H. B. ELLWANGER. With an Introduction by GEORGE H. ELLWANGER. 12mo, cloth, 5s.

THE GARDEN'S STORY; or, Pleasures and Trials of an Amateur Gardener. By G. H. ELLWANGER. With an Introduction by the Rev. C. WOLLEY DOD. 12mo, cloth, with illustrations, 5s.

THE KINGDOM OF GOD IS WITHIN YOU. Christianity not as a Mystic Religion but as a New Theory of Life. By COUNT LEO TOLSTOY. Translated from the Russian by CONSTANCE GARNETT. Library Edition, in 2 vols, crown 8vo, 10s. Also a Popular Edition in 1 vol., cloth, 2s. 6d.

THE OLD MAIDS' CLUB. By I. ZANGWILL, Author of "The Bachelor's Club," &c. With Illustrations by F. H. TOWNSEND. Crown 8vo, 3s. 6d.

WOMAN—THROUGH A MAN'S EYE-GLASS. By MALCOLM C. SALAMAN. With Illustrations by DUDLEY HARDY. Crown 8vo, 3s. 6d.

FROM WISDOM COURT. By H. S. MERRIMAN and S. G. TALLENTYRE. With 30 Illustrations by E. COURBOIN. Crown 8vo, 3s. 6d.

THE GENTLE ART OF MAKING ENEMIES. By J. M'NEILL WHISTLER. *A New Edition.* In One Volume, pott 4to, 10s. 6d.

THE WORKS OF HEINRICH HEINE.

Translated by CHARLES G. LELAND, F.R.L.S., M.A. The Prose Works in Eight Volumes. In cloth cabinet price £2 10s., or separately 5s. per volume. Volume I., Florentine Nights, Schnabelewopski, The Rabbi of Bacharach, and Shakespeare's Maidens and Women. Volumes II. and III., Pictures of Travel. In Two Volumes. Volume IV., The Salon. Volumes V. and VI., Germany. In Two Volumes. Volumes VII. and VIII., French Affairs. In Two Volumes.

THE FAMILY LIFE OF HEINRICH HEINE.

Illustrated by one hundred and twenty-two hitherto unpublished letters addressed by him to different members of his family. Edited by his nephew Baron LUDWIG VON EMBDEN, and translated by CHARLES GODFREY LELAND. In One Volume, 8vo, with 4 Portraits. 12s. 6d.

DE QUINCEY MEMORIALS.

Edited by ALEXANDER H. JAPP, LL.D., F.R.S.E. In Two Volumes. Demy 8vo, with Portrait, 30s. net.

THE POSTHUMOUS WORKS OF THOMAS DE QUINCEY.

Edited by ALEXANDER H. JAPP, LL.D., F.R.S.E. Volume I. Suspiria de Profundis and other Essays. Volume II. Conversation and Coleridge, and other Essays. Crown 8vo, 6s. each.

The Great Educators.

Each subject complete in one volume.
Crown 8vo, price 5s. each.

ARISTOTLE, and the Ancient Educational Ideals. By THOMAS DAVIDSON, M.A., LL.D.

LOYOLA, and the Educational System of the Jesuits. By Rev. THOMAS HUGHES, S.J.

ALCUIN, and the Rise of the Christian Schools. By Professor ANDREW F. WEST, Ph.D.

FROEBEL, and Education by Self-Activity. By H. COURTHOPE BOWEN, M.A.

ABELARD, and the Origin and Early History of Universities. By JULES GABRIEL COMPAYRÉ, Professor in the Faculty of Toulouse.

Others in preparation.

New Six Shilling Volumes.

THE HEAVENLY TWINS. By SARAH GRAND, Author of "Ideala," &c.

IDEALA. By SARAH GRAND.

OUR MANIFOLD NATURE. By SARAH GRAND. With Portrait of the Author.

A SUPERFLUOUS WOMAN.

THE STORY OF A MODERN WOMAN. By ELLA HEPWORTH DIXON.

THE LAST SENTENCE. By MAXWELL GRAY, Author of "The Silence of Dean Maitland," &c.

APPASSIONATA: A Musician's Story. By ELSA D'ESTERRE-KEELING.

FROM THE FIVE RIVERS. By FLORA ANNIE STEEL, Author of "The Potter's Thumb."

RELICS. Fragments of a Life. By FRANCES MACNAB.

THE TOWER OF TADDEO. By OUIDA.

THE O'CONNORS OF BALLINAHINCH. By Mrs. HUNGERFORD, Author of "Molly Bawn."

THE KING OF SCHNORRERS, GROTESQUES AND FANTASIES. By I. ZANGWILL. With over Ninety Illustrations.

CHILDREN OF THE GHETTO. By I. ZANGWILL.

THE PREMIER AND THE PAINTER. A Fantastic Romance. By I. ZANGWILL and LOUIS COWEN.

THE RECIPE FOR DIAMONDS. By C. J. CUTLIFFE HYNE.

THE COUNTESS RADNA. By W. E. NORRIS.

THE NAULAHKA. A Tale of West and East. By RUDYARD KIPLING and WOLCOTT BALESTIER.

AVENGED ON SOCIETY. By H. F. WOOD, Author of "The Englishman of the Rue Cain."

Heinemann's International Library.

Edited by EDMUND GOSSE. Price 3s. 6d. cloth, 2s. 6d. paper.

** Each Volume has an Introduction specially written by the Editor.

New Review.—"If you have any pernicious remnants of literary chauvinism, I hope it will not survive the series of foreign classics of which Mr. William Heinemann, aided by Mr. Edmund Gosse, is publishing translations to the great contentment of all lovers of literature."

Times.—"A venture which deserves encouragement."

IN GOD'S WAY. From the Norwegian of BJÖRNSTJERNE BJÖRNSON.

PIERRE AND JEAN. From the French of GUY DE MAUPASSANT.

THE CHIEF JUSTICE. From the German of KARL EMIL FRANZOS, Author of "For the Right," &c.

WORK WHILE YE HAVE THE LIGHT. From the Russian of COUNT TOLSTOY.

FANTASY. From the Italian of MATILDE SERAO.

FROTH. From the Spanish of DON ARMANDO PALACIO VALDÉS.

FOOTSTEPS OF FATE. From the Dutch of LOUIS COUPERUS.

PEPITA JIMÉNEZ. From the Spanish of JUAN VALERA.

THE COMMODORE'S DAUGHTERS. From the Norwegian of JONAS LIE.

THE HERITAGE OF THE KURTS. From the Norwegian of BJÖRNSTJERNE BJÖRNSON.

LOU. From the German of BARON VON ROBERTS.

DOÑA LUZ. From the Spanish of JUAN VALERA.

THE JEW. From the Polish of JOSEPH IGNATIUS KRASZEWSKI.

UNDER THE YOKE. From the Bulgarian of IVAN VAZOFF.

FAREWELL LOVE! From the Italian of MATILDE SERAO.

THE GRANDEE. From the Spanish of Don ARMANDO PALACIO VALDÉS.

Popular 3s. 6d. Novels.

ACCORDING TO ST. JOHN. By AMÉLIE RIVES, Author of "The Quick or the Dead."

ORIOLE'S DAUGHTER. By JESSIE FOTHERGILL, Author of "The First Violin," &c.

THE MASTER OF THE MAGICIANS. By ELIZABETH STUART PHELPS and HERBERT D. WARD.

THE HEAD OF THE FIRM. By Mrs. RIDDELL, Author of "George Geith," "Maxwell Drewett," &c.

THE STORY OF A PENITENT SOUL. Being the Private Papers of Mr Stephen Dart, late Minister at Lynnbridge, in the County of Lincoln. By ADELINE SERGEANT, Author of "No Saint," &c.

NOR WIFE, NOR MAID. By Mrs. HUNGERFORD, Author of "Molly Bawn," &c.

THE HOYDEN. By Mrs. HUNGERFORD.

MAMMON. A Novel. By Mrs. ALEXANDER, Author of "The Wooing O't." &c.

DAUGHTERS OF MEN. By HANNAH LYNCH, Author of "The Prince of the Glades," &c.

A LITTLE MINX. By ADA CAMBRIDGE, Author of "A Marked Man," &c.

A MARKED MAN: Some Episodes in his Life. By ADA CAMBRIDGE.

THE THREE MISS KINGS. By ADA CAMBRIDGE.

NOT ALL IN VAIN. By ADA CAMBRIDGE.

A KNIGHT OF THE WHITE FEATHER. By TASMA, Author of "The Penance of Portia James," "Uncle Piper of Piper's Hill," &c.

UNCLE PIPER OF PIPER'S HILL. By TASMA.

THE PENANCE OF PORTIA JAMES. By TASMA.

Popular 3s. 6d. Novels.

THE SCAPEGOAT. By HALL CAINE, Author of "The Bondman," &c.

THE BONDMAN. A New Saga. By HALL CAINE.

CAPT'N DAVY'S HONEYMOON, The Blind Mother, and The Last Confession. By HALL CAINE.

THE RETURN OF THE O'MAHONY. By HAROLD FREDERIC, Author of "In the Valley," &c. With Illustrations.

IN THE VALLEY. By HAROLD FREDERIC. With Illustrations.

THE COPPERHEAD, and other Stories of the North during the American War. By HAROLD FREDERIC.

KITTY'S FATHER. By FRANK BARRETT, Author of "The Admirable Lady Biddy Fane," &c.

MR. BAILEY-MARTIN. By PERCY WHITE.

A QUESTION OF TASTE. By MAARTEN MAARTENS, Author of "An Old Maid's Love," &c.

COME LIVE WITH ME AND BE MY LOVE. By ROBERT BUCHANAN, Author of "The Moment After," "The Coming Terror," &c.

A ROMANCE OF THE CAPE FRONTIER. By BERTRAM MITFORD, Author of "Through the Zulu Country," &c.

'TWEEN SNOW AND FIRE. A Tale of the Kafir War of 1877. By BERTRAM MITFORD.

Popular Shilling Books.

PRETTY MISS SMITH. By FLORENCE WARDEN, Author of the "The House on the Marsh," &c.

MADAME VALERIE. By F. C. PHILIPS, Author of "As in a Looking-Glass," &c.

THE MOMENT AFTER. A Tale of the Unseen. By ROBERT BUCHANAN.

CLUES; or, Leaves from a Chief Constable's Note-Book. By WILLIAM HENDERSON, Chief Constable of Edinburgh.

Dramatic Literature.

THE PLAYS OF ARTHUR W. PINERO.
Price 1s. 6d. each paper cover, 2s. 6d. cloth.
I. The Times. II. The Profligate. III. The Cabinet Minister. IV. The Hobby-Horse. V. Lady Bountiful. VI. The Magistrate. VII. Dandy Dick. VIII. Sweet Lavender. IX. The Schoolmistress.

THE MASTER BUILDER. A Play in four Acts. By HENRIK IBSEN. Translated by EDMUND GOSSE and W. ARCHER. Small 4to, with Portrait, 5s. Popular Edition, paper, 1s.

BRAND. A Dramatic Poem in Five Acts. By HENRIK IBSEN. Translated in the original metre with an Introduction and Notes by C. H. HERFORD. Small 4to. 7s. 6d.

HEDDA GABLER. A Drama in Four Acts. By HENRIK IBSEN. Translated by EDMUND GOSSE. Small 4to, with Portrait, 5s. Vaudeville Edition, paper, 1s.

*** A limited Large Paper Edition, with three Portraits, 21s. net.

THE FRUITS OF ENLIGHTENMENT. A Comedy in Four Acts. By LYOF TOLSTOY. Translated from the Russian by E. J. DILLON. With an Introduction by A. W. PINERO, and a Portrait of the Author. Small 4to, 5s.

THE PRINCESS MALEINE. Translated from the French by GERARD HARRY; and **THE INTRUDER.** By MAURICE MAETERLINCK. Translated from the French. With an Introduction by HALL CAINE. Small 4to, with a Portrait. 5s.

THE LIFE OF HENRIK IBSEN. By HENRIK JÆGER. Translated by CLARA BELL. With the Verse done into English from the Norwegian original by EDMUND GOSSE. In One Volume, crown 8vo, 6s.

A COMMENTARY ON THE WORKS OF HENRIK IBSEN. By HJALMAR HJORTH BOYESEN, Author of "Goethe and Schiller," "Essays on German Literature," &c. Crown 8vo, cloth, 7s. 6d. net.

---

21 BEDFORD STREET, LONDON, W.C.

www.ingramcontent.com/pod-product-compliance
Lightning Source LLC
Chambersburg PA
CBHW031728230426

43669CB00007B/289